KT-151-067

Mental Health and the Community

**REPORT OF THE
RICHMOND FELLOWSHIP ENQUIRY**

© 1983 The Richmond Fellowship

ISBN 0 9503473 1 0

Published by Richmond Fellowship Press
8 Addison Road, Kensington, London W14 8DL

Price: £2.50

Printed by Green & Co. (Lowestoft) Ltd., Crown St., Lowestoft. Suffolk

CONTENTS

THE RICHMOND FELLOWSHIP ENQUIRY INTO COMMUNITY APPROACHES TO THE MENTALLY ILL

The Rt. Hon. the Earl of Longford, K.G., P.C., (*Chairman*)
Former Leader, House of Lords.

*Ms. Elly Jansen, O.B.E., (*Deputy Chairman*)
Director, The Richmond Fellowship.

*The Rt. Hon. the Earl of Beswick, P.C.,
Former Chairman,
British Aerospace.

*Mr. Kenneth Coleman,
Divisional Director,
Social Services Department,
City of Westminster.

The Baroness Faithfull, O.B.E.,
Former Director,
Social Services Department,
Oxfordshire.

*Dr. John Horder, C.B.E., F.R.C.P.,
F.R.C.PSYCH.
Past President,
Royal College of General Practitioners.

Mr. Vaughan Jones,
Co-ordinator,
New Horizon Youth Project,
Drury Lane, London.

Professor Kenneth Rawnsley, M.B.,
CH.B., F.R.C.P., P.R.C.PSYCH.,
President,
Royal College of Psychiatrists.

*†The Lord Redcliffe Maude, G.C.B.,
Independent Member,
House of Lords.

The Lord Richardson, M.V.O., M.A.,
M.D., F.R.C.P.,
Former President,
General Medical Council.

Mr. Peter Thompson, M.I.P.R.,
F.INST.D.,
Honorary Director,
The Matthew Trust.

The Baroness Trumpington, J.P.,
Penal Reform Committee,
House of Lords.

*Professor John Wing, PH.D., M.D.,
F.R.C.PSYCH.,
Institute of Psychiatry,
University of London.

The Lord Winstanley, M.R.C.S.,
L.R.C.P.,
Former Chairman,
The Countryside Commission.

Mr. Willem van der Eyken (*Secretary*).
Development Officer, Richmond Fellowship.

*Member of the Drafting Committee.
†Deceased November 20, 1982.

ACKNOWLEDGEMENT

A grant of £5,000 from the Nuffield Foundation to cover the expenses of the Enquiry is gratefully acknowledged.

PREFACE

This Enquiry resulted from a debate in the House of Lords, initiated by Lord Longford, about the care, or lack of care, for those among us who suffer from the particularly distressing and disabling conditions collectively known as mental illness.

Statistics show that one woman in five and one man in nine will require psychiatric treatment at some time in their lives. During this year an estimated one million people will receive some psychiatric care. Yet, though the need is so demonstrably widespread, there is a marked reluctance to accept social responsibility for providing resources to meet that need. There was agreement, shared by this Enquiry, in the House of Lords debate of 31 March, 1981, that the present policy of broadening district-based services to provide alternative care for people hitherto living in the larger mental hospitals was correct. But though the government spokesman then said that hospital places had been reduced from 143,000 in 1954 to 76,000 in 1979, he was unable to show that the necessary alternative services had been provided.

It seemed clear that a new impetus was needed if necessary progress was to be made. Accordingly, some Peers who took part in that debate, together with others representing a range of relevant interests and expertise, joined in this Enquiry. Lord Longford was elected Chairman, Ms. Elly Jansen, Deputy Chairman, and Mr. Willem van der Eyken, Secretary. The membership of the Enquiry is listed on page v.

It was decided to concentrate attention on adult mental disorders other than mental handicap and dementia. Conditions such as alcoholism and drug addiction, important though they are, were also excluded. Since the rundown in mental hospital places has been more rapid in England and Wales than in Scotland or Northern Ireland, the Enquiry focused its attention principally on England and Wales. Nevertheless, the principles enunciated are applicable to the whole of the United Kingdom. The Enquiry has covered a broad spectrum of interests. Members have talked to those who have suffered from mental illness and to relatives, nurses, social workers, psychiatrists, general practitioners, community physicians, voluntary workers, administrators and planners.

This Report endeavours to establish facts in what is a very complex medical and social field. It sets out in its recommendations a community framework designed to bring together the contributions of the National Health Service, the local authorities and the voluntary agencies.

It asks for a government Minister with clear responsibility for the development and maintenance of defined standards of mental health care. It emphasises the need for a new Development Fund to make a reality of proposed community services.

The truth is that hitherto our society has found it difficult to appreciate the needs of the mentally ill. In the national and local authority budgets, the provision for their care has never been adequate. Private generosity has responded less readily to the appeal of the emotionally and mentally disturbed than to almost any other good cause.

It is right to pay tribute to those who have felt called to work in this field, either in the public services or the voluntary agencies. It is imperative to recognise, however, that they now need additional resources.

It is hoped that this Report will increase understanding and stimulate informed discussion, and that pressure of public opinion will help ensure that real progress is made towards the mental health service here proposed.

SYNOPSIS

When the services and other forms of help provided for people afflicted with mental disorders are compared with the problems these people and their relatives now face, large gaps and serious inadequacies are found. The picture is not wholly black. Good services do exist and good ideas for innovation abound. The dominant impression, however, is one of disappointment. This Report describes the situation frankly but only with a view to elucidating remediable factors. The conclusions and recommendations are thus based firmly on current experience and are possible of achievement within the foreseeable future.

An overview of the Report may be obtained by reading the short summaries at the ends of Chapters 1 to 9, and Chapter 10, which contain the recommendations. This synopsis provides a briefer outline.

The origins of the present imbalance between a mental hospital system that is running down and an alternative system that is not being built up at anything like an equivalent rate are traced in Chapter 1. Chapters 2 and 3 provide a non-technical description of the major kinds of severe mental disorder and of the more common problems of 'mental ill-health' respectively. The Report has addressed itself chiefly to the former. Chapter 4 summarises the present sad state of statutory services for mentally ill people or those at risk.

These first four chapters raise the question of what constitutes good 'community care'. Some examples of initiatives that appear highly promising are mentioned in Chapter 5. They include a charity concerned with the welfare of people with schizophrenia and their relatives, a community psychiatric nursing scheme, two unusual day centres and a 'drop-in' centre, a voluntary agency that runs forty therapeutic communities, and a rehabilitation workshop. Many other examples could be given, both from the statutory and from the voluntary sector. The latter deserves special attention and Chapter 6 is devoted to a consideration of the ways in which charitable organisations can contribute to the welfare of people with mental disorders. Their potential has not yet been sufficiently exploited.

On the basis of the material considered in the first six chapters, members of the Enquiry set out in Chapter 7 three principles of good community care: district responsibility, comprehensive coverage and continuity of care.

District, or geographical, responsibility means that local statutory

ix

services, with the help of voluntary organisations and support from well-disposed local groups, should identify and meet the need for services for the mentally ill within their district. At the moment, the responsibility is divided between different authorities and agencies.

Comprehensive coverage means that a wide variety of provision is necessary in order to meet local need. The elements required are listed on pp. 60—63. At the moment even the inadequate minimal levels laid down in the Government White Paper of 1975 for certain types of care have not been reached, nor do they appear likely to be achieved, at present rates of progress, during this century.

Continuity of care means coordinating services to meet constantly changing needs; at individual, family, unit and district level. At the moment this principle is more honoured in the breach than the observance.

Considerable attention is given to the way in which a District Mental Health Service could be better organised and managed in order to meet these standards of good community care. Arrangements are suggested that would provide individuals and families with help and guidance through the maze of health and welfare services, ensure better communication and coordination between service units while giving each one more managerial independence, and provide a flow of relevant information to a Joint Mental Health Development Committee, comprising senior representatives of the health and local authorities and voluntary agencies. Such Committees should be given the responsibility for achieving at least the minimal quantitative standards for the district services laid down in the White Paper, which should be given statutory force, and for improving their quality. They should also be given certain financial duties as specified below.

Members of the Enquiry were impressed by the way Her Majesty's Inspectors of Education have raised the general level of education in this country and thought that the nucleus of such a system at present provided by the Health Advisory Service and the Social Work Service Officers for Regions should be augmented and directed towards similar ends.

It is very unlikely that substantial improvements in local mental health services can be expected unless there is also a general improvement in the training of staff, geared to the principles of good community care. Attention is directed, in Chapter 8, to the training of psychiatric nurses and social workers, but the principles apply equally to other mental health professions.

In Chapter 9, the fundamental question of paying for a good system of community care is considered. About £700m. was spent on services for patients residing in mental illness hospitals and units in 1980–81. By contrast, only about £110m. was spent on health and social service provisions such as out-patient clinics, day care, non-hospital residential care and field social work for the mentally ill. The present joint funding arrangements, whereby NHS funds can be diverted to other community projects, are not satisfactory because local authorities or voluntary organisations have to take over the revenue costs after a 'tapering' period of seven to thirteen years. This they are increasingly reluctant to do.

It is therefore suggested that new local Mental Health Development Committees should be created and given responsibility for identifying the present 'mental health budget' spent by Health and Social Service Authorities in their Districts, comparing the figures with the levels of service provided and with expenditure in other Districts, and eliciting explanations from health or local authorities that are not meeting minimal standards. The reports of the Inspectorate would be valuable here. The Committees would also be responsible for administering the present joint funding arrangements.

These arrangements would not, however, allow for the development of good community care along the lines proposed without the allocation of further financial aid, particularly in districts of special need, such as inner city areas where there is a substantial proportion of 'single homeless' people. A new Development Fund is therefore necessary. This cannot be provided from the transfer of resources from the run-down of hospitals, nor from the realisation of their assets, since there will be a long time lag before it is clear how much will eventually become available in this way. Substantial annual investment of additional funds must be made available by central government over a considerable period of time. This could be disbursed through present 'joint funding' arrangements, with the proviso that revenue costs should, in special cases, be continued indefinitely.

Each Joint Mental Health Development Committee should make bids for support from the Development Fund but would be unlikely to be successful if its current mental health budget was unjustifiably lower than elsewhere. An annual scrutiny of this budget would also prevent the use of Development Fund monies to replace commitments previously accepted by local health or social service authorities.

These recommendations require that one of the Department of Health and Social Security ministers, assisted by a Departmental Planning Board, should be identified as having special responsibility for the allocation of the Development Fund for generally improving the Mental Health Service.

The recommendations arising from the detailed argument of Chapters 7, 8 and 9 are brought together in Chapter 10. Rather than attempting to summarise them further, it is suggested that they should be consulted directly.

Finally, members of the Enquiry are well aware that substantial areas of mental disorder have not been covered in this Report; notably mental handicap, severe mental infirmity in elderly people, alcoholism, drug abuse, and the mental disorders of childhood and adolescence. The exclusion of these topics does not indicate any lack of awareness of their importance. On the contrary, it is suggested that each needs equivalent examination in its own right and that similar principles to those enunciated here may well be found to apply throughout.

1 WHY SHOULD THE COMMUNITY CARE?

Introduction

Most of us, when asked what we want from life, will put health near the top of our list of priorities. We would also like a secure home, good personal relationships, a satisfying occupation, absorbing interests, an adequate income. All these are put at risk if we become sick or disabled and, conversely, failure to achieve these objectives can predispose to ill-health. Of all the catastrophes that can afflict us in this way, none is as distressing or alienating as mental illness. One woman in five and one man in nine will require psychiatric treatment at some time in their lives. Nearly everyone, therefore, will have some experience of mental illness, either in themselves or in a near relative.

Unlike most other forms of illness, however, mental illness carries a social stigma that further disables those afflicted, embarrasses the relatives and others who want to help, and leads to a tacit avoidance of the subject (except for disparaging jokes) by the population at large. This is not a promising basis for politicians and administrators to build on.

When it is recalled that about one per cent of the population are in touch with psychiatric services on any given day (nearly a half of them actually in-patients) and that a further one per cent will make contact during the ensuing year, making altogether a million people in a population of 50 million, and that this excludes those in need who are not receiving specialist help, the sheer scale of the problem can begin to be appreciated. Because of the failure to provide adequate care outside hospital, there are still some residents who stay simply because of the lack of alternatives, while many of those who have been discharged remain at risk of being re-admitted.

But it is not just those who are afflicted who need help. Their relatives often have to carry the burden imposed by inadequate community services.

How can such a situation have arisen? In order to answer this question, it is necessary to understand the lines along which the mental health services have developed up to now.

The first era of reform

The neglect of the mentally ill has a long history.[16] During the early years of the nineteenth century in England, pauper lunatics were dealt

1

with by parish overseers under the old Poor Law, others went to prison (since there was no diminution of responsibility because of insanity), others were confined under the vagrancy laws in the local bridewell or house of correction, others were sent to private madhouses where they had virtually no legal protection, a few were treated in Bethlem Hospital (hence the term 'bedlam'), and a substantial number were confined alone in 'single care', often chained in coal-cellars or other out-of-the-way corners. The general assumption was that the able-bodied unemployed or destitute deserved their fate. Very little attempt was made to distinguish between the 'impotent' or handicapped and 'sturdy rogues or vagabonds'. All tended to be herded into the same work-houses, where living conditions depended upon local charity and the quality of the overseers. Under the 1834 Poor Law Amendment Act, everyone receiving public assistance had to be in a workhouse. Congregated among the destitute were the handicapped, the chronically sick and the old.

The first public mental hospitals were set up in reaction against these intolerable conditions. Charitable reformers and pioneering doctors began to campaign for new laws and for new provisions specifically for the mentally ill and retarded. Small county asylums began to be established, most of which provided markedly better conditions than work-houses and private madhouses, and some of which were outstandingly good for the time. Most had acres of grounds, including home farms. The legal provisions were poor, however, making no stipulations about treatment, but imposing penalties if a patient escaped.

The early pioneers advocated 'moral' treatment—education, work and an ordered and well-disciplined regime—rather than bleeding, purging and the use of restraints. An atmosphere of optimism about the curability of mental disorders prevailed. The discharge rates were as high as those reached to-day. Charles Dickens, who had been appalled by the conditions in London workhouses, was greatly impressed by a small hospital he visited in the United States, where the physician and staff sat down to dine with their patients.

The custodial era

Unfortunately, the era of reform did not last, partly because the pioneers had been too optimistic and it began to be clear that the claims for cures had been exaggerated; partly because of new problems created by the growth of industrialisation; and partly because the earlier campaigns had been too successful. Larger and larger numbers of people were admitted. The carefully fostered family atmosphere of the small asylums could not be maintained as the wards became over-crowded and under-staffed. The Lunacy Acts of 1890 and 1891, which codified and systematised the various legal restrictions on the freedom of the mentally ill, required at least one certificate of unsoundness of mind or mental defect and an order by a justice at the time of admission. The laws were interpreted so strictly that only severe, chronic and probably incurable cases could be accepted. Much of the impetus towards the development of a comprehensive system of services, based on the principles of humane social care, was lost. Before the end of the nineteenth century, the 'custodial' era had arrived.

Given the twin facts of a large patient population, all under compulsory orders, and a small, inadequately trained, staff, it was inevitable that procedures adopted for the control of a few potentially dangerous or disturbed patients should be generalised to the relatively amenable majority. Routines of supervision and control were developed which would leave nothing to chance; hence the railed airing-courts, the small-paned or barred windows that would open only two inches and the warning whistle that every attendant carried. Hence, too, the almost impenetrable barriers between the self-sufficient institution and the outside world. Staff and inmates came to have stereotyped views about each other, all sorts of institutional rituals developed out of the reward and punishment systems and a special jargon became the symbol of an isolated and secret society. Outside the walls, public attitudes became indifferent so long as the laws were strict enough to ensure that improper detention did not occur and the institutional security was tight enough to ensure that residents did not escape.

This description paints the blackest picture. It was not all black. But the custodial era in the mental hospitals deeply affected the attitudes of the general public and of those with a special interest in the care of the mentally ill. The remnants of those attitudes—for, against and indifferent—are with us still. One of the major effects was that the longer an individual had been resident, the more used he or she became to the hospital regime and the less likely to want to adventure out into the world again. This 'institutionalism' itself reinforced the whole system.

A new era of reform

The pendulum of opinion began to swing back after the first world war when the first attempts were made to dismantle the Poor Law system and to begin developing the 'Welfare State'. The Mental Treatment Act of 1930 broke the stranglehold of the Lunacy Acts; people could at last be admitted without a compulsory order. Following the second world war, the process accelerated, with the passing of legislation on pensions, family allowances, education, provision for the disabled, a complex of social services and the establishment of a National Health Service. The mental hospitals were incorporated, with the general hospitals for the acutely ill and the hospitals for the chronic sick, into one system.

Many of the mental hospitals were too large, had unsuitable buildings, were remote from the districts they served and encumbered by a long history of stigma, pauperism, institutionalism and neglect. Nevertheless, the late 1940s and the 1950s saw a tremendous change in atmosphere in the pioneering hospitals: from pessimism to optimism, from idleness to activity, from custody to treatment and from institutional to a community orientation. The introduction of useful forms of medication in the mid-1950s gave extra impetus to these changes. The new drugs were particularly helpful in controlling the most severe symptoms of acute mental illness and therefore in reducing the length of time that patients had to remain in hospital.

Perhaps the most important element for longer-stay patients was the introduction of methods of social and vocational rehabilitation and resettlement and the development of the view that many patients were disabled rather than ill. Paid work was provided for long-stay patients instead of diversionary arts and crafts or maintenance work on the institution. Hospital farms were sold because it seemed, at the time, that they could lead to exploitation of people who were quite fit enough to be discharged but who might be retained because they were good workers. Locked doors were opened and transitional environments of various kinds were provided in order to provide a ladder back to full community life. At the same time there was an emphasis on early discharge in order to avoid the disabilities of institutionalism.

From 1954 onwards the number of beds occupied in the English mental hospitals began to decline, from 344 per 100,000 population at the end of 1954 to 171 per 100,000 at the end of 1978. The number of beds was approximately halved, to about 80,000, during that time. (The numbers in Scotland and Northern Ireland have always been higher and the decline less rapid.) This change was due partly to a decrease in the length of time that patients stayed following admission and partly to the discharge of people who had been in hospital for many years.

By 1960, the government was formulating plans based on the eventual closure of the large mental hospitals, with acute treatment being given exclusively in small local psychiatric units attached to District General Hospitals. The remaining functions, both for short-term and for long-term care, would be carried out 'in the community'.

Bringing together the three sections of the NHS (the public health service, the hospital service and the general practitioner service) and trying to base hospital care on Health Districts which, in general, conform to local authority boundaries, prepared the way for such a development. On the other hand, the social services with the main responsibility for non-hospital care are administered by local authorities and, with the aid of large non-earmarked grants from central government, are also funded locally. The NHS, in general, is well-regarded even by the taxpayer, so that there is no great public pressure for cuts in the care provided, including care for the mentally ill. By contrast, the obligation of local authorities to provide alternative residential and day care is not so well understood or accepted. Joint care arrangements, whereby NHS funds could be diverted for a time to help establish facilities which eventually would be taken over by local authorities, proved useful. However, as the deadlines for the local government to take over approached, the financial problem looked as difficult as ever. The new forms of service that would deliver the necessary care in the community were not sufficiently provided.

During the 1960s and 1970s another factor undoubtedly influenced events. This was the development of a significant section of opinion which regarded the psychiatric services themselves as creating disability and the staff of hospitals as doing little more than adding medical labels to problems which were essentially social in nature. The effect of this labelling process, it was suggested, was to divert the focus of care away from social agencies into hospitals, where dependence could only be increased. There was some basis for this idea in the old custodial system; indeed, hospital psychiatrists were the first to document it and to pioneer reforms. But the reaction was excessive and contributed to an over-optimistic view that the mental hospitals could be closed without an undue burden being placed on other types of service. Further consideration of the current state of knowledge about mental illness and the most effective methods of treatment and care will be found in Chapter 2.

The present situation

At present, therefore, the psychiatric services are in a state of imbalance. On the one hand, the large hospitals are half run down and changes have taken place in the hospital system that make it difficult for them to discharge many of their functions, particularly those which are social rather than medical. The hospital farms have been sold off; the hospital shops and entertainments and functions are more and more difficult to keep going (and may be regarded as fostering dependency); staff who used to live in houses on the hospital grounds, sometimes following a family tradition over several generations, are now hard to come by; some staff feel that a 'therapeutic atmosphere' is impossible unless only people capable of 'informed consent' are admitted, thus excluding many mentally ill people who could benefit from treatment; some hospitals no longer have the capability to cope with seriously disturbed patients, creating the necessity to set up special 'secure' units, involving even greater stigma and difficulties in staffing; finally, the concept of the hospital as an *asylum* or refuge of last resort has lost appeal.

These functions of the large mental hospital have not, however, been taken over by alternative non-hospital services. In so far as shelter, asylum, security, basic nursing and care are still required on a long-term basis, albeit for a smaller group of people than formerly, it is now difficult to find appropriate places. The wide range of substitute provisions—hostels, group homes, subsidised housing, domiciliary supervision, day centres, rehabilitation and sheltered workshops—has not been established on an adequate scale and the current climate, both financial and vocational, is not favourable. Social Services Departments are competing for scarce funds and have to allocate their slender resources according to their own priorities, among which the mentally ill have a lowly place. The voluntary organisations do their utmost to meet the need, but their resources, too, are severely limited. Where services are inadequate, the relatives and the afflicted have to cope as best they can.

The picture is not, however, one of unrelieved gloom. As we shall show in subsequent chapters, all the elements of a decent service for the mentally ill do exist somewhere in the country. What we do not find is a single district where all the necessary elements are combined together in a properly functioning mental health service. Although it may take a decade or more to create a system of recognition, treatment and care that will cater appropriately for the needs of the mentally ill, there is sufficient evidence of good practice to make recommendations that could substantially alleviate the problems that now exist. We shall suggest in Chapter 9 that additional government funds are essential to facilitate the transition towards a system that will end the pendulum swing from inadequate community care to inadequate institutional care and back again.

In the next chapter, we consider the problems posed by the severe mental illnesses and the knowledge recently accumulated concerning the best methods of prevention or amelioration. It is on this knowledge that the planning of adequate services must rest.

Summary

Although nearly everyone puts his or her own health (including mental health) close to the top of a list of personal priorities, those who become afflicted by mental disorders join a group which is accorded the lowest priority for care by the health and social services of our so-called welfare state. This neglect is not a new phenomenon. It has persisted for centuries.

During the past century and a half there have been two great eras of reform. The first was initiated in reaction against the appalling conditions in the workhouses and madhouses of early Victorian England. But the small asylums that were then set up, inspired by the ideas of moral treatment and non-restraint, developed eventually into the long restrictive 'custodial era'. After the second world war the pendulum began to swing the other way. The numbers in the institutions began to decline and the ideal became care 'in the community'.

Now, however, we have reached a point of crisis. Governments of all persuasions have accepted responsibility for maintaining the national health service, the social services and the basic infrastructure of the welfare state. They have applauded and fostered the run-down of the large institutions.

The answer to the question, 'Why should the community care?', is that, not only the impetus, but much of the progress made during the second era of reform may be lost unless a further drive is made towards establishing adequate arrangements, without recourse to large institutions, for those who cannot provide for themselves because they are afflicted by severe mental disorders. The backlog of neglect and indifference must be corrected in order to enhance the dignity, value, sense of responsibility and fulfilment of mentally ill people. Since there is a price to pay for this, we must remember Oliver Wendell Holmes' remark: 'Taxes are the price we pay for a civilised society.'

2 SEVERE MENTAL ILLNESS. THE NATURE AND SIZE OF THE PROBLEM

The concept of 'need'

The problem with most discussions of 'need for services' is that they are carried on at several removes from the difficulties experienced by individuals; often being concerned only with the numbers of hospital beds or day places or other resources 'needed'. Such questions are, of course, important, and we shall return to them, but it is first necessary to consider more fundamental issues.

We mentioned briefly, at the beginning of Chapter 1, the kinds of thing that most people want from life—security, love, friendship, health, interesting and useful occupations, material sufficiency, and so on. Human hopes and expectations vary markedly from one culture to another, and even within one apparently homogeneous country, but good health is near to the top of almost everybody's list anywhere in the world. Without it, most of the other aims are immensely more difficult to achieve or maintain. Severe mental illnesses are often disproportionately distressing and socially disabling compared with more familiar diseases because they affect the emotions and the reason. The first priority therefore is to try to understand them and the factors that influence them for better or worse in order to be able to make rational suggestions about how to help those who are affected.

In addition to ill-health (and often precipitating it as well as being caused by it) there is social disadvantage—stigma, a lack of social supports, poverty, and paucity of vocational or social skills. As a further complication, a loss of self-confidence and self-esteem often leads to a lowered capacity to cope with adversity and decreases the level of adjustment likely to be achieved. Mental illnesses are particularly likely to be accompanied by social disadvantages and under-achievement.

Knowledge about the nature of severe mental illnesses, and of social disadvantages and adverse personal reactions, provides a solid basis on which to investigate methods of prevention, treatment, restitution and care. It is only when we have identified the frequency of the clinical and social problems within a given population, and thus determined how many are in need of various forms of care, that we are really in a position to consider the size of provision of services. Services exist to 'deliver' the most appropriate forms of care to people in need. No one has a need for services, as such, only for a particular combination of forms of care.

It is essential to understand this underlying logic in order to see that even if the Government's guidelines on numbers of places in non-hospital services (day centres, workshops, hostels, group homes, etc.), or on numbers of nurses or social workers or doctors per 100,000 population, were fulfilled (which, in general, they are not), it would not necessarily mean that the needs of the individuals in contact with those services were being met. Everything depends on how well the services are performing their functions. A further conclusion is that different patterns of service may be equally good, or bad, at meeting the needs of a community. It may not be necessary for every district to have an identical pattern to every other in order to meet needs for care.

Finally, we cannot avoid the question of cost. If two different patterns of service are equally effective in meeting need for care, the one that is more economical is to be preferred. Some needs may be considered too expensive to meet on a large scale. Others may not seem to have high priority in one culture, but are thought to be extremely important in others. Financial support depends on such factors. The fact that some services may meet need more economically than others suggests that running services more effectively does not necessarily cost a great deal more money. Large sums are already being spent on mental health services (including £700 million on in-patients and £150m. on other forms of care—see Chapter 9). However, changing from a less effective to a more effective pattern may require substantial capital investment. Consider what the Victorians invested in their institutions.

This analysis demonstrates the complexity of the concept of need, but it shows that the basic principles are quite simple to interpret given sufficient knowledge about the extent of social disablement in the population. We do, in fact, know quite a lot about the disablement associated with mental illnesses and this knowledge will be summarised in the next three sections.

Schizophrenia

If we exclude from present consideration those severe mental disorders with a clear-cut organic cause or pathology, like dementia and mental retardation, and those connected with the abuse of alcohol or drugs, undoubtedly the most severe disorders and the ones most likely to lead to prolonged residence in hospital are the schizophrenic and paranoid psychoses. Because of their severity and chronicity, these disorders dominate the provision and deployment of specialised psychiatric services. About one person in a hundred can be expected to suffer from such a condition at some time during their lifetime. At any given moment about three people in every thousand are receiving treatment or care from one of the specialist services because of schizophrenia; 165,000 in the population of the United Kingdom.

It is hard to appreciate what an acute episode of schizophrenia is like, and the problems created for patients and relatives. Those afflicted have extraordinary and frightening experiences, far worse than those of a nightmare because the individual is fully awake, which affect the very centre of their mental lives—the way they think. Thoughts may seem to be loud or distorted, or divided into those which are recognisable and under control and those which seem to have their origin elsewhere. This is the origin of the 'voices' of which so many complain. The will seems to be replaced by that of some other agency so that the individual does not feel in control of actions or speech. These experiences are real, not imaginary.

Once we understand what these strange experiences are like, we can also appreciate that it is, in a way, quite natural to try to explain them in terms of paranormal or physical forces being directed at mind and brain—telepathy, ghosts, radio-waves or X-rays. It is also possible to see why so many people think that a deliberate attempt is being made to harm them. The explanations may be extremely bizarre and, if acted upon, the resulting behaviour is incomprehensible to those who do not know what the individual is going through. One of the major problems is that 'insight' may be lost completely; the individual can no longer use ordinary standards of 'reality' against which to judge what is happening.

Fortunately, this acute condition usually improves quite quickly with treatment and is then often forgotten, just as dreams are. But the threat of relapse remains. There is a further difficulty; some patients also develop longer-term disabilities—slowness, under-activity, poverty of speech and a marked difficulty in using non-verbal means of communication. Taken together these problems mean that the patients may become very withdrawn socially; behaviour that can be interpreted as laziness or unfriendliness by those who do not recognise the 'invisible disabilities'.

We now know that both kinds of symptom tend to vary according to the circumstances in which the individual is living. Relapse can be precipitated by various kinds of stress—particularly too high expectations, for example by too vigorous efforts at rehabilitation or socialisation, or too much criticism from a close relative or friend who does not understand the nature of the disabilities—and by the kinds of adversity to which everyone is subject from time to time, but to which schizophrenic patients are particularly vulnerable. A degree of shelter, including a degree of social withdrawal, may therefore be protective. On the other hand, an under-stimulating environment, such as used to be common in the 'back wards' of some large and under-staffed hospitals where patients spent long hours doing absolutely nothing, and which may still be observed in some hospitals and some of the non-hospital alternatives, can lead to a damaging increase in long-term disability and loss of self-esteem and confidence.[28]

People suffering from schizophrenia, apart from those few (about twenty per cent) who make a good recovery, therefore have to walk a tight-rope, trying to avoid the dangers of too much stress on one side and too little activity on the other. It is no wonder that so many fail to find a balance or that so many relatives are at a loss to know how to help. Relapse with acute symptoms is one of the commonest causes of admission to hospital. On the other hand, although only about four per cent of all those admitted remain in hospital as long as a year (i.e. become 'long-stay') compared with two thirds during the 1930s, social disablement is quite common. Those afflicted may not achieve the educational and vocational level that would otherwise be expected, may not have many close personal relationships, may not marry and may live rather restricted and solitary lives. These people are socially disabled.

In relation to hospital care, there are three main problems. First, more than half of the present hospital population consists of people admitted because of a schizophrenic breakdown many years ago, who are growing old there. A substantial proportion has reached retirement age while in hospital. Second, a small but very significant group still becomes long-stay in hospital in spite of all efforts to prevent this; the so-called 'new' long-stay. Most are severely disabled. Third, those who leave hospital often have some degree of long-term disability and also remain at risk of acute relapse and re-admission—they are therefore in need of prolonged 'after-care'. Many of these are living at home with relatives, who complain that the care received is often thoroughly inadequate.[18]

'Our son, with a good honours degree in economics, was in the middle of an established career when he began to deteriorate for no known cause and became unable to manage the details of his everyday life. He was then 27 years old. Since then, he has been living with us for six years, with two spells in hospital. We are both in our seventies, but have been unable to have any relief from his care. We are unable to go away except when he can go to his brother for one or two weeks in the year. What he needs is confidence and support, and the company of young people, as well as understanding of his illness.'

Fortunately, as people with schizophrenia get older, the intensity of the 'positive' symptoms—leading to delusions and hallucinations—often decreases. Moreover, some patients and relatives learn (perhaps more by trial and error than by education from professionals) to 'live with schizophrenia', to recognise and avoid situations that cause relapse, to manage medication sensibly, to keep active and develop new interests, to make full use of such opportunities as are available in day centres and sheltered workshops, to look after themselves and to help other people understand their difficulties. Many, however, do not have such opportunities or cannot make use of them. They leave home and live solitary, unproductive and uncomfortable lives. The suicide rate is high in this group and so is the risk of complete destitution, as is shown by studies of people who 'live rough' or sleep in Reception Centres or night shelters.[17]

James was found one night by a worker from a charitable organisation sleeping in a cardboard box 'under the arches' near Waterloo station. He was completely confused but accompanied the worker willingly enough to a night shelter. Later he was found a place in a small home with other men who had been destitute. It transpired that he had been in and out of several mental hospitals but had no relatives, was incapable of work and could not even care properly for himself. He remained solitary and needed much reminding to get up in the mornings, keep himself clean and so on, and he talked to himself a great deal. But he seemed contented in his new life and looked a different person.

Although the medical treatments and other methods of care available are by no means perfect, sufficient knowledge has accumulated to help increasing numbers of people to live lives of decent quality at home or elsewhere and to minimise both risk of relapse and the severity of long-term impairments. We shall consider the implications of this knowledge for planning services later (see Chapter 7).

Mania and severe depressive illnesses

After schizophrenia, the principal condition accounting for long-term residence in hospital, and for prolonged contact with community services outside hospital, is depression. Severe depressions are sometimes associated with episodes of mania, in which the afflicted individual experiences the opposite of an abnormally depressed mood, and is actually elated. This may not appear, at first sight, to be a very serious problem because, when most of us experience elation, it is due to some particularly satisfying experience that we would want repeated. Elation in mania, however, has an unpleasant edge to it, and is accompanied by seriously disturbing symptoms such as over-activity, sleeplessness, grandiose ideas that are impossible of achievement but nevertheless influence action, and loss of the ability to judge the actions of self and others (particularly relatives and close associates) except in terms dictated by the abnormal emotional state.

People who have episodes of severe depression and of mania are said, because of the opposite poles of emotion that they experience, to be suffering from 'bipolar' disorders. Severe depressions, accompanied by other disabling symptoms—slowness, underactivity, insomnia, loss of weight, feelings of exaggerated guilt and lowered self-esteem with a high risk of suicide—also occur quite often without any history of mania. The various combinations—mania, depression and manic-depressive illness—are given the collective name 'affective disorders'.

Compared with schizophrenia, affective disorders are often relatively short-lived. Early treatment with recently discovered forms of medication terminates the acute disorder rapidly, although lesser problems can remain for some time thereafter. What is required is early recognition, admission to hospital if disturbed behaviour makes this advisable, and prompt treatment. Relatives and patients come to recognise the first signs of an episode but, if the stage when a patient is willing to have treatment passes, insight may be lost and there is then no alternative to compulsory admission. Such decisions may be difficult to make and it is important for the public to understand why.[26]

A man was brought to the emergency clinic of a psychiatric hospital because his wife said he was over-active, elated and sleepless and was beginning to speak of spending their joint savings on some totally unrealistic scheme. She thought his judgement totally irrational. She also feared violence if she crossed him, although this was not her principal worry. On two previous occasions similar symptoms had developed into full-blown mania but, because he convincingly denied abnormality when seen by doctors, he was not compulsorily admitted before he had ruined their small business. He had responded quickly to treatment on both occasions and the marriage had otherwise been very satisfactory. Now his wife pleaded that he be admitted in time to prevent it all happening a third time. The man was in control of himself during the interview, denied all symptoms and refused admission. The psychiatrist thought compulsion could not be justified and he was not in fact admitted for another week, during which time he again spent all their savings.

Manic-depressive disorders are responsible for more admissions to hospital than schizophrenia but, because of the more rapid and complete response to treatment and the lower risk of long-term damage to personality and the capacity to form personal relationships, the length of stay is shorter and the outcome, in general, more favourable. Nevertheless, 16 per cent of the 'new' long-stay in hospital* have been given a diagnosis of affective disorders, second in frequency only to schizophrenia, and this is also true of people in other forms of sheltered residential setting or day centres.

*See Chapter 4 for discussion of 'new' long-stay.

One of the reasons for this accumulation is that those affected remain liable to relapse after discharge, a disadvantage analogous to the 'invisible' disabilities of schizophrenia. If they have experienced several such relapses ('short-cycle' disorders) they may themselves become unwilling to leave hospital even though they are apparently free from severe symptoms. Lack of confidence, which may result in part from a persisting depressive disorder of lesser severity, may be responsible for this. Much then depends on the alternatives available as the following example suggests.

A woman of forty-five had experienced frequent attacks of severe depression and made several attempts at suicide. Her husband had left her because of this. She was admitted each time to a hospital where she felt secure but, after discharge, even when she had gone to an after-care hostel (where most of the residents were younger than herself) she had relapsed under only mild stress. Now in hospital for eighteen months and free of depressive symptoms, she nevertheless does not wish to leave. She has friends in the hospital and uses the hospital facilities, but the staff feel that she is too dependent. What she needs is a supportive hostel where she can feel part of the community but also have a more independent life; perhaps eventually moving to an apartment on her own but with social support. No suitable hostel is available in the area.

As in schizophrenia, social disadvantages and adverse personal reactions need as much attention as the symptoms themselves and the position of relatives requires similar support. For a vulnerable person to learn how to cope with everyday stress can be far more difficult than most of us who are relatively healthy recognise. The common advice—'pull yourself together'—may be cruel mockery to someone perilously close to the edge of a severe nervous breakdown. 'After-care' is more, therefore, than the offer of shelter in the form of day care or a place in a hostel (though these can sometimes be very helpful and may prevent the necessity for further hospital admission). After-care also means providing help to live as normal a life as possible within one's own limitations.

Other disorders leading to use of psychiatric services

Although schizophrenia and the affective disorders are the principal diagnoses (other than dementia, organic illnesses and mental retardation) given to people using the psychiatric services, accounting for more than 80 per cent of those in contact on any given day, a number of other conditions need to be considered. These include severe forms of anxiety and phobic states, obsessional neuroses, personality disorders, alcohol abuse and addiction to various drugs.

Anxiety states, even when severe, can often be treated successfully. Sometimes, however, phobic states can become intractable. One man, for example, was so frightened of travelling and of mixing with other people that for years he could not leave his home. Psychotherapy and behaviour therapy were ineffective. His wife left him. He now lives in a single room and walks to a day centre where he works slowly but conscientiously. He is completely solitary and his principal need is for a social club. Fortunately, this is an unusual outcome.

Obsessional states are more frequently unresponsive to treatment. A young unmarried man had for years had to carry out complicated mathematic calculations in his head, over and over again, in spite of everything he tried to stop it. He also had to carry out all sorts of routines, always in precisely the same order, which meant, for example, that he took two hours or more to prepare for bed. He was completely incapacitated and only felt relief when, his distress becoming intolerable, he was admitted to hospital for a time.

Personality disorders and over-indulgence in alcohol may complicate other diagnoses. One woman aged 60 lived alone in a council flat and attended a day centre. She had married at 18 a man who spent most of the next twenty years in prison. She suffered from tension and 'nerves', becoming depressed when things went particularly wrong, and was admitted to hospital on innumerable occasions, each time leaving after a few weeks. She drank more and more and now has binges lasting as long as she has money to buy alcohol. She is very demanding and difficult with neighbours, and at the day centre, which she attends erratically. She quarrels constantly and noisily with her husband when he is at home. Her health is in danger because of the high alcohol intake.

In some cases, the only label that seems appropriate is 'inadequate personality'. An unmarried woman of 36 has two children. One aged 15 is the subject of a care order and boarded out with foster parents; the other was adopted at the age of 6. All her life she has lived hand to mouth. A series of men-friends have moved into her council flat, often bringing their own friends, and she has sometimes been turned out to walk the streets while they held parties. She is not able to judge her own interests. When each crisis arrives she gets desperate and asks to be admitted to hospital. She has attempted suicide several times. On other occasions she has been abusive and violent to neighbours and to relatives and twice has been admitted to hospital on police orders. She rarely stays in hospital long; after a few days she returns to the same round.

These few examples illustrate some of the difficulties faced by services. Failures cannot always be put down to lack of will or of facilities to help. Indeed, sometimes very substantial resources (statutory and voluntary) are made available over a long period of time without obvious result. However, the outcome is not always so relentlessly intractable. Many of the people referred to psychiatric services, even when their difficulties seem just as complex, do find the help they need. It should also be recognised that people are often, and appropriately, referred because the diagnosis is unclear or because their behavioural problems seem to have no obvious organic or social explanation. A substantial proportion of referrals result in just one out-patient consultation, following which a letter of comment is sent to the general practitioner but no specialist treatment or care is recommended. These problems, and those very common ones which do not result in referral at all, will be considered in Chapter 3.

However, patients discharged from hospital, or their families (often themselves distressed), do usually contact general practitioners during the subsequent year. The action needed may be prescription of medication, arrangements for admission, referral to other services or just the offer of sympathy and support. The relatives of people with schizophrenia always speak most warmly of a family doctor who has been kind during their adversity and who has tried to arrange for the right kind of care. Another service they value is that of community psychiatric nurses who are most effective when working both with general practitioners and with psychiatrists. It will be suggested in Chapter 4 that many people with chronic psychiatric disorders, and their relatives, have physical as well as mental problems. The assessment of physical health is the responsibility of the family doctor, as is advocacy for specialist health and social services.

Mentally ill Offenders

A further small but very important group must also be considered because, although it spans the whole range of diagnoses, it gives rise to specially difficult problems that are frequently misunderstood. This is the group of 'mental offenders'—people who are recognised as mentally ill while they are before the courts or after they are sent to prison for some offence. They may remain in prison, or be sent to psychiatric hospitals or special hospitals under the terms of the Mental Health Act. During 1981, 300 patients were either discharged from special hospitals or transferred to ordinary psychiatric hospitals.

After discharge from hospital, such a person may remain a 'marked man'. Landladies, voluntary organisations, the DHSS, the police and potential employers, may regard him with fear and distress. Some offenders can be regarded by society as having paid for their crimes by imprisonment and as deserving of a chance to demonstrate that they have reformed. But mental illness often carries the implication of a further breakdown, and further unpredictable crimes. This, in addition to the fact that prison and hospital provide for all the inmates' immediate requirements, (there being no need to earn a living and the standard of amenities sometimes being higher than would be achievable outside), may partly account for the relatively high relapse rate.

The first year after release is a crucial period, when proper provisions for gradual rehabilitation can reduce the problems of security so important to the general public, and give the individual an opportunity to restore self-confidence, renew skills and put down new social roots.

Similar after-care problems arise when the mental illness of offenders is not recognised and they serve the sentence in prison, or when the recommendations of court or prison doctors for transfer to hospital are unavailing because no place can be found. Lack of 'availability' is not always due to shortage of beds; it may arise from the reluctance of staff to accept people who might be disruptive of the 'therapeutic community' or justify any stigma already attached to the hospital by the local community.

It is reasonable to accept that an individual should not be regarded as insane if the evidence of severe mental illness is not strong. When the evidence is obvious, however, it is unjust if appropriate treatment and care is not forthcoming.

Forms of Care

The enormous range and complexity of need has been described in this chapter as frankly and realistically as possible. The complexity arises not so much from the fact that there are innumerable types of mental illness; compared with the rest of medicine there are few. The problem lies in the way that mental disorder is manifested in the infinite variety of human personality. The kinds of care needed can however be characterised under a few headings—prevention, medical treatment, social and vocational training, education, counsel, supervision, support, security, welfare and shelter. When we come to examine, in Chapter 4. the present state of services, the standard by which they are judged will be whether all these forms of care are available in each district and, if so, whether they are effectively being 'delivered' as and when needed by individuals and their families.

Summary

People afflicted by mental disorders share many problems. Social disadvantages such as stigma, a lack of social supports, poverty, unemployment and isolation may be due to the illness and may also precipitate it. A loss of self-confidence and self-esteem often leads to an even poorer capacity to cope with difficulties that are already severe enough.

Different disorders also give rise to more specific patterns of disability. After dementia and mental retardation, the most severely handicapping condition is schizophrenia. An acute breakdown is not only terrifying and alienating for the individual who experiences it but shocking and frightening to onlookers. Acute schizophrenia comes closest to the ordinary person's idea of madness. Chronic schizophrenia, however, is characterised by slowness, underactivity and social withdrawal. Although many people recover, it is those who do not who remain in long-term need of help and care.

Mania and severe depression are more understandable because they represent exaggerations of the normal moods of elation and depression. When severe, however, they too are seriously disabling and, in some people, breakdowns occur at frequent intervals, leaving little time to recover confidence and social functioning in between times.

Other conditions leading to referral for psychiatric advice and help include severe forms of anxiety and phobic states, obsessional neuroses, personality disorders, alcohol misuse and addiction to various drugs.

A brief description of each of these conditions is given in order to illustrate the specific problems that arise and the forms of care that are needed. The problems shared by people with severe mental disorders, many of which are also shared by those with severe physical disabilities, mental retardation or dementia, are also described.

3 THE COMMONER MENTAL DISORDERS AND THE PRIMARY CARE SETTING

Mental Ill-health in the general population

The major concern of the Enquiry is with the standard of care available to people who have been discharged from hospital but still have problems or who are at high risk of hospital referral if their problems are not relieved. Some 1 per cent of the population are newly referred to out-patient clinics or are admitted to hospital during the course of a year because of the conditions described in the last chapter. However, a much larger proportion experience psychological symptoms which, although usually of much lesser severity compared with such disorders as schizophrenia, can nevertheless be severely distressing and at times disastrous.

For example, about 15 per cent of us, if asked about our mental state in a community survey, complain of excessive worrying, nervous or muscular tension, anxiety, irrational fears, depression or irritability. It is doubtful whether most of these common disorders should be regarded as illnesses—perhaps 'mental ill-health' is a better description—but they do often lead to consultation with a general practitioner. The person affected commonly complains of a physical symptom such as backache, headache, loss of weight or insomnia, and the psychological problems have to be elicited.

The role of the general practitioner

Only about 5 per cent of consultations with a family doctor result in referral to a psychiatrist and these represent the most severe disorders.[23] The specialist services could not cope with a higher proportion of referrals. It therefore falls to the general practitioner to recognise mental ill-health, whether represented openly or in disguised form; to give it due importance, to listen and to help—sometimes by discussion, sometimes by medication for anxiety or depression, sometimes by giving practical advice, sometimes by personal support during a crisis or over longer periods of time.

It might be assumed that early attention to the milder disorders would lead to prevention of more severely disabling conditions like schizophrenia, but there is little evidence to support this.

Nevertheless, those who suffer from mental ill-health do need help, sometimes urgently as in the case of deliberate self-poisoning—the commonest means used in so-called 'suicidal attempts'. (The *intention* to commit suicide is often absent.) Problem drinking (i.e. repeated drinking that leads to social, psychological or physical problems) has been calculated to occur in over one per cent of adults and also causes difficulties in family members.[20] Significant psychological problems in the parent(s) are found to be present in about half the consultations with general practitioners about children.

A difficulty with many of the problems in this group arises from the complex way in which 'inner' factors create difficulties in the family, at work and in other relationships, and how these difficulties, in turn, create a vicious circle.

An anxious working class mother sought help from nine agencies about her husband's drunken habits. In each case she was offered sympathy and help in the form of getting people to talk to the husband. A counsellor at the tenth port of call helped her to talk about her own worries. It transpired that she was concerned lest her daughter, then in her late teens and going out with boys, should become pregnant. The mother had herself become less interested in sex and her husband had reacted by frequenting the pub. Although she said he was unco-operative, after discussing her worries, she relaxed sufficiently to persuade him to attend the agency. He was reserved, but not unhelpful when he realised he was not going to be cast in the role of scapegoat. Both partners were able to recognise how they had contributed to the problem and, through a more happy relationship to each other, were able to give their daughter more support and security.

Doctors and counsellors are familiar with the way in which some of their clients, with skilled help, can disentangle their emotional problems so that the presenting (apparently practical) problem can be more effectively resolved.

Mental ill-health is often the result of adverse psychosocial circumstances. The depression that follows bereavement (which is, of course, normal, not abnormal) is an obvious example. But poverty, poor housing, physical or mental disorder in a member of the family, an unsatisfactory marriage, lack or loss of social supports, difficulties at work, the threat or actuality of redundancy, are all forms of adversity which may result in severe psychological distress. The emotional reaction may then in turn exacerbate the social problems. In a way, such reactions can be regarded as normal. It is true, however, that some people are more vulnerable to such reactions than others, who appear to be able, for a variety of reasons (including upbringing, personality, variety of social skills, etc.) to cope with such adversity as fate throws in their way. We are concerned here with people who suffer severe psychological distress with consequent social disablement.

A young mother of three children, one of them recently before a juvenile court for shoplifting and another severely mentally retarded, had been deserted by her husband. The rent of her dilapidated flat was in arrears and she had been threatened with eviction. The pills prescribed by her family doctor had not relieved her constant worrying, sleeplessness and depression. Eventually, she took an overdose of the pills and was admitted to a general hospital, her children being taken into care. She 'recovered' rapidly and was then discharged. She needs urgent social help, support and counsel.

Anyone who comes into contact with people under stress will be familiar with these problems but if such people get into touch with statutory services it is likely to be with their family doctors. A recent report from the Royal College of General Practitioners discussed the best means of help and prevention.[19] It was emphasised that knowledge is still limited but that anticipatory guidance before crises or life changes occur (such as childbirth, divorce, major surgery, bereavement, retirement, etc.) supportive intervention during and after the event, early treatment and appropriate referral when necessary, is often beneficial.

It is often useful to involve specialist professionals—psychiatrists, nurses, social workers and psychologists—in the general practice setting and this is facilitated by health centres, shared by a group of family doctors, where there is space for such activities. Liaison with self-help groups is also a great advantage.

One such group practice in north London comprises six general practitioners, supported by health visitors, district nurses, community psychiatric nurses, social workers, marriage guidance counsellors and psychiatrists. Some 25 professional people are involved from time to time. Although this is not a typical arrangement, it shows that collaboration between agencies can be achieved at the level of primary medical care. Since nearly three quarters of general practitioners now work in practices of two or more there is plenty of opportunity for development.

Such an approach is more expensive and it is a point of concern that the share of resources allocated to general practice has declined by comparison with the hospital services. The increased proportion of medical students opting for general practice (up from one fifth to more than a third) is unlikely to be maintained unless the importance of primary care is recognised in practical terms.

A range of community support services is needed, such as walk-in centres, refuges, social clubs and recreation centres, which do not bear a medical or social work label. Examples will be found in Chapter 5. General practitioners and social workers would be able to improve their own service substantially if they were supplementing such community help instead of substituting for it.

Mental health education

Education should, of course, begin at home and be given form in school. In particular, as children become adolescent they can begin to understand, through their own personal problems and developing sense of identity, how others, too, feel and think and make their individual contribution to the school's community life. Fifth and sixth formers need to be helped towards a sense of their responsibility to each other. The school organisation can facilitate this by bringing pupils into consultation and providing for realistic experience of decision-making and problem-solving at all levels, from form meetings to school 'parliaments'. Sources of help for personal problems should be well known and accepted. The standard of pastoral care available will depend, in part, on the emphasis given to it during the primary training of staff.

Another obvious channel for mental health education is provided by the churches. Clergy are in a good position to run discussion groups of people contemplating marriage, or recently married, or parents, or others with problems in common. Some church communities already draw upon the strengths of their congregations in order to help members who are in emotional or social difficulties. This spiritual and practical sustenance can sometimes prevent psychological distress from developing into serious breakdown.

The provision of individual counselling and community social work in key housing estates is another way to counter alienation and hopelessness. Fortunately, the lesson that tower blocks, or schemes with no personal outside space for which householders are responsible, breed serious social problems, vandalism and crime, has now been learned. But many such estates still exist. Susan Holland ran an Action and Counselling Centre in Battersea which, in terms of its aims of helping local people 'to combat the mental and material sufferings of everyday life', was very promising.[14] The sad fact is that such schemes are not readily funded.

The Barclay Report recommended that social service departments should co-operate with housing, health and education services, with a view to building up shared responsibility and decreasing dependency.[1] 'The notion of a community implies the existence of a network of reciprocal relationships which, among other things, ensure mutual aid and give those who experience it a sense of well-being. An important feature of community is the capacity of the networks of people within it to mobilise individual and collective responses to adversity.'

In support of such local efforts the national awareness also needs to be heightened. The media can play a particularly important part here; social and economic policies should be informed by charity, in the widest sense of the word, since the concept of service requires that the stronger should help the weaker and the more affluent should support those less endowed than themselves.

Summary

This chapter is concerned with the common emotional disorders that surveys show afflict about 15 per cent of the population at any one time. Although not necessarily linked to the severe disorders with which this Report is chiefly concerned, 'mental ill-health' on this scale reflects common social and interpersonal problems that can cause severe personal distress and lead to heavy use of the health and social services. General practitioners, in particular, are likely to be consulted. Suggestions are made concerning the role of family doctors, social workers and other counsellors.

Mental health education and community support, in schools, places of work, church communities, and deprived settings such as some inner city housing estates, can help to lessen the impact of adversity and to foster independence.

4 COMMUNITY CARE IN ACTION

The concept of community

The term 'community' is used in several different ways. A convenient definition is a geographically and administratively defined area, such as a borough or county, where the responsibility for providing 'community care' is entrusted to statutory health and social authorities, with back-up from housing, welfare, employment and voluntary services.

Another meaning of 'community' is a relatively well-integrated district or neighbourhood, where the inhabitants know each other and few local residents need feel isolated or remote from help should they need it. Perhaps few neighbourhoods nowadays are communities in this sense, as many were when villages and townships were smaller and more self-sufficient than most are now. Nevertheless, the idea of 'integration' is often inherent to some extent in the use of the term 'community'. It is felt, for example, that disabled people should, as far as possible, be helped to use public amenities and facilities, to live in ordinary houses, to undertake the same activities, and to receive the same personal support from friends, relatives and neighbours as those who are physically and mentally fit.

Sometimes this concept is used in a related but different sense to mean communities specially created to foster personal relationships between a group of people with a common purpose, as in a religious community, a therapeutic community or a sheltered community, although this usage does imply some degree of segregation from the general population. Such a 'community of interest' can include those with mental or physical disorders such as blindness, physical disabilities or mental illness.

Finally, the narrowest and most negative usage, which we deplore but which is unfortunately fashionable, is to define 'community' in terms of any form of living other than inside hospital. The quality of life 'in the community' is regarded as intrinsically superior, so that discharge from hospital or prevention of admission is approved irrespective of the alternative. A policy based on this assumption can lead to even less satisfactory care than was provided in hospital. A need for hospital care is only lessened if adequate alternatives are made available. If these alternatives are not provided, or are withdrawn, a need for hospital care will be reasserted. What hospitals were trying to do, albeit inadequately, must still be done.

24

We have adopted the first definition (i.e. district responsibility), qualified by the view that the aim of services should be to foster and promote community living in the second sense, (i.e. integration with local informal support systems), so far as this is possible. Special aids should be supplied to supplement the ordinary resources of the community in helping mentally disabled people to live as normal a life as is possible. In this chapter we shall consider how far statutory health and social services are actually achieving this aim at present.

The delivery of community care

The needs for care outlined in the previous chapters demand a whole complex of services, covering:

the early identification of people in need;

prompt assessment of the problems requiring help, repeated as necessary;

prescription and long-term supervision of medication;

advice to patient and relatives about physical health and the management of positive and negative symptoms;

the provision of a continuum of residential units providing various degrees of shelter, support and challenge, ranging from hospital wards, through staffed hostels and unstaffed group homes, to supervised lodgings, supportive housing and bed-sitters;

a similar spectrum of day units, from day hospitals, through occupational therapy and industrial therapy centres, to sheltered workshops or specially created conditions in open industry;

help with welfare rights and benefits, obtaining education, vocational training and decent housing;

social clubs, dinner clubs and other forms of support during the leisure hours and weekends.

We have emphasised earlier that the simple provision of a service does not necessarily mean that needs for treatment or care are being met. Indeed, as history shows, both community and hospital services can actually do harm. Much depends also on the deployment and co-ordination of services and on staff ratios and staff training, subjects which are considered in more detail in Chapters 7 and 8. The essence of the matter is that staff must be able to identify problems and provide the most effective methods of prevention, treatment and care. If they can do this, the precise pattern of services through which they 'deliver' the care is of less importance, unless there are differences in cost.

In the following sections we shall consider whether the services now provided, at the halfway stage in the run-down of the large mental hospitals, are actually meeting need.

The statistical context

Table 1 is presented in order to provide a context for this review and for the chapters to come. It shows how the numbers resident in English psychiatric hospitals on 31 December each year have been declining during the past decade. The figures are taken from the annual statistical reports published by the Department of Health and Social Security and are given separately for three sub-groups: those in hospital for less than one year, for one to five years, and more than five years, on the given days. The trend in Wales is similar.

Table 1

ENGLISH MENTAL HOSPITALS AND UNITS

Resident patients on 31 December, 1966 and 1970–78,
by length of stay

Rates per 100,000 total population

	1 year	1–5 years	5 + years	Total
1966	71	194		265
1970	66	167		233
1971	64	47	116	227
1972	62	44	109	215
1973	62	41	102	205
1974	58	40	96	194
1975	59	39	90	188
1976	58	39	84	181
1977	57	40	78	175
1978	57	39	75	171

N.B. Peak total rate in 1954 was 344 per 100,000

It can be seen that the total number resident at the end of 1978 was 171 per 100,000 population (a total of about 80,000 people), a number that has been steadily declining since the peak in 1954.*

The decline is most obvious among those who have stayed more than five years, now down to 75 per 100,000 or 44 per cent of the total, although two-thirds (and probably more) of the annual decrease is due to death rather than to discharge. The large question is whether better quality accommodation could be provided and at what cost.

The middle group, resident between one and five years, has been

---

*The rate varies widely in different parts of Europe and North America, depending on local circumstances and traditions and the availability of alternative services. The Scottish figure is about twice as high as the English. Some countries, such as Finland, have much higher rates even than Scotland.

declining in numbers but seems to have reached a steady level of about
40 per 100,000 population. Over half are more than 65 years old.
Nowadays, only about 5 per cent of all patients admitted to hospital
stay as long as a year but this small proportion accumulates. The
government plan to provide local hospital care only for 'acute' disorders would mean that the longer-stay group would have to live in
acute wards in district general hospitals.

The third sub-group (about 60 per 100,000 population) is composed
of patients who have been in hospital for less than a year. Most stay
only a few weeks and spend nearly all their time 'in the community'.
The obvious problems, therefore, apart from the question of preventing
admission in the first place, arise from the needs for 'after-care'.

These three hospital sub-groups provide a starting-point for studies
of need. The next two sections deal with the problems of long-stay
hospital patients and of patients discharged from hospital after a short
stay.

Long-term care in hospital

Table 1 shows that 44 per cent of the people in mental hospitals have
been in-patients for more than five years; often they have been resident
for twenty years or more, having grown old there. Patients tend to be
single or 'post-marital', middle-aged to elderly, with few social roots in
a community, few work skills, and frequent previous admissions to
hospital. Nearly half have been diagnosed as suffering from schizophrenia and many have multiple (including physical) disabilities. Few
have a strong desire to leave hospital. Schizophrenia is the commonest
diagnosis. The hospital provides housing, activity in occupational
therapy departments or workshops, leisure opportunities and large
grounds. The occupational and recreational facilities are variable but
can be quite good. Accommodation is rarely in houses though large
villas are available for less disabled people. Most hospitals cannot be
called sheltered communities in the sense, for example, of the 'villages'
set up by the Steiner organisation. However, in the case of hospitals
sited far from the districts they serve, the difficulties in the way of using
public amenities and facilities and participating in the everyday life of
the neighbourhood seem very difficult to overcome.

On the credit side, some hospitals are sited within their own districts
and contain the potential for development as true sheltered communities and for integration as one part of the overall pattern of local
medical and social services. One pioneering hospital proposed that part
of its grounds should be used to build a local authority housing estate;
a few houses for patients and staff, some for the local population.
Unfortunately, this eminently sensible idea did not come to fruition.

Much depends, however, on the size of any new accumulation of recently admitted patients. Table 1 shows that nearly a quarter of mental hospital beds are used by patients who have been resident between one and five years. This is a very substantial proportion and it raises the question whether alternative provision could be made for such people. If so, it would reduce recruitment of the 'adult mentally ill' to the over-five-year group.

Studies in which 'new' long-stay patients were interviewed to discover their problems and wishes, together with the views of hospital and local authority staff, suggest that many patients could be accommodated in supervised hostels and attend day centres, although travel between the two could give rise to problems. Some patients are not only suffering from mental illness, but are also physically disabled, elderly or mentally retarded; they would often need specialised care. Unfortunately, because of the severity of the mental disability (particularly slowness, poor self-care, disturbed behaviour, security problems, risk of relapse, etc.) local authority and voluntary organisations are rarely willing to accept responsibility. Hospitals, as the statutory agencies, cannot refuse, hence the accumulation.

If hospitals are within easy reach of the districts they serve, and if they were to take on the characteristics of a true sheltered community, they could cater for this group in houses set up on site, with the front door opening on a public road and the back door opening on to sheltered grounds, and with a variety of daytime and leisure-time activities available both within and outside the hospital boundaries. One such 'hospital-hostel' has been established and has worked very well.[27] Others are now being set up and evaluated. There may be other solutions to this crucial planning problem, equally deserving of evaluation. In districts where there is no local accommodation for long-stay patients some other solution (for example, a couple of large houses with shared gardens) *must* be provided, possibly by the District Health Authority, by the local authority Social Services Department, or by a voluntary organisation.

Gaps in aftercare

Studies of the needs of people discharged from hospital, and of their families, reveal substantial gaps in services.[3] Some relatives say that they were not even informed that the discharge would take place and that they and a partially recovered patient were left entirely without help. They would have welcomed someone who could give guidance about how to cope with disturbed behaviour or self-neglect or social withdrawal and point out how to minimise the risk of relapse or possible attempts at suicide. It is true that relatives sometimes find out by trial and error what is the best approach, but the experience of failure, even if it leads eventually to success, can be demoralising and disheartening. This is the time when family break-up can occur.

Preventing unnecessary admission to hospital should be one of the functions of the community services. Some people could be admitted directly to day hospital so long as full support is given at home. Others need 'retreat' rather than treatment—they just want space and time to think out their problems without being under immediate stress. Some need the kind of environment supplied by a Richmond Fellowship hostel (see Chapter 5). Others can be treated at home without any need for day or residential care.

Relatives often report difficulty in getting practical advice of the kind that could prevent admission. It is rarely appreciated by staff that they stand in for relatives when caring for patients. The odd or disturbed behaviour that they are professionally trained to cope with in specially equipped surroundings and for limited periods of time, relatives have to cope with alone, at home, often with no advice or support.[18]

> One patient was discharged from hospital and lay on his bed all day, not bothering to wash or dress. His parents had no idea what they should do. They contacted the psychiatrist who told them to be permissive and let their son do as he pleased. He became more and more inert, finally becoming incontinent. He was re-admitted when he stopped eating. The hospital nurses, who were used to coping with these problems, gave the parents some useful advice which made things much easier after discharge.

The opposite difficulty—getting a patient into hospital when admission really is needed—is also described. (See example on p. 13.) The general practitioner has primary responsibility. 'Crisis intervention' teams are useful for dealing with emergency problems, as are medical and social walk-in centres. Rapid action requires coordination of general practitioner, hospital and social services. At the moment, such teams are only available in a few districts.

Out-patient clinics are available nearly everywhere, but they are overcrowded and there is rarely time to discuss problems in the detail that is needed. It may be difficult for a relative to get an appointment since the psychiatrist may feel committed to his patient and be unwilling to breach 'confidentiality' in order to discuss methods of management. What should be done about someone who does not take medication as prescribed? How should side-effects be coped with? Is there any way of anticipating and preventing further breakdown? Usually there is little time even for the patient to discuss these matters. The interview may last no more than a few minutes. A frequent complaint is that the doctor is a junior under training who changes every six months or so and thus cannot get to know the circumstances.

Getting help in an emergency—particularly in the evening and at weekends—is frequently mentioned as being troublesome. The general practitioner can be a great help if he has been in prolonged contact with the family, is well-informed by the specialist and has a clear idea of the various services available locally. Sometimes, however, family doctors are reluctant to intervene and relatives may be told that they are over-anxious and left to cope on their own.

A young man had been very disturbed and smashing windows. His parents called the doctor. The man was very suspicious about the visit, wanting to know what the doctor had come for and what was in his bag. The doctor told the parents there was nothing he could do as the patient did not appear to be in active danger. He said he had other patients to attend to and left hastily.

One of the most helpful services is provided by the community psychiatric nurse, who can visit at home as well as at a clinic, who knows the individual and family well and can provide assistance in emergencies. However, many districts do not have a service of this kind and few families benefit from it at the moment.

The social services do not fill the gap. They are under even greater pressure, trying to tackle a multitude of problems with declining resources. Mental illness is not a high priority compared, for example, with problem families, the physically disabled or the elderly. Families may not be given the advice and help they need about welfare arrangements and benefits that would make the difference between poverty and a bare sufficiency. Even the understanding of real problems and the support in the face of adversity that makes a difficult situation easier to bear may not be forthcoming.

Another important gap is in the provision for leisure time. If sufficient day places are available, patients at least have something to do during the weekdays though, as things stand at the moment, they are rarely using their capacities to full potential. However, the leisure hours, long and empty for those who live alone, stretch out every evening and weekend. It is at such times that breakdowns commonly occur. Voluntary organisations are most useful here—befrienders, restaurant and social clubs, outreach from churches and other organisations. Catering for one is expensive, shopping on a limited budget is an ordeal (particularly for those whose specific disability is slowness and difficulty with concentration), 'cheap' cafe meals are often inadequate in quality and quantity. Walking the streets can be as soul destroying as sitting alone in a room. Self-help systems such as the

Psychiatric Rehabilitation Association provides in Tower Hamlets are a valuable but rare facility.[2]

When, as occasionally happens, all these services are available and working well, the social difficulties presented by severe mental illness are ameliorated and the individuals and their relatives are enabled to cope. Many people do recover from severe mental illness and are pleased with the care they have received. However, it is clear to members of the Enquiry that services generally fall woefully short of achieving the quality of life for the mentally ill and their families that was envisaged when the run-down of the large hospitals began with such a fanfare. During the transition from care in large institutions to care distributed between many small local units, staffed by professionals with little training in common who need not be in close touch with each other, the problem of overall coordination has not received sufficient priority. Even within one administrative hierarchy such as a District Health Authority or a Social Services Department each small centre tends to develop its own traditions, select its own clients, guard its own autonomy and deny responsibility for what happens elsewhere. We do not yet have a true 'mental health service' (see Chapter 7).

Residential care outside hospital

Studies of people living in staffed hostels, unsupervised group homes and boarding-out schemes show that they have similar characteristics to those who become long-stay hospital residents, except that they are less severely impaired. Most have been admitted to hospital, often several times, and have been in contact with psychiatric services over many years. Over half have been given a diagnosis of schizophrenia.

It was feared, at one time, that such accommodation might become like 'back wards in the community', under-stimulating and restrictive in regime and just as isolating in effect. In fact, recent surveys[22] have been reassuring in this respect, although group homes (houses shared by a few residents with no resident staff) may not receive much attention from visiting staff. Residents can become very underactive and far from being integrated into the local community. When shared by people who are not too disabled and have reasonable social skills, group homes provide an opportunity for independence and a base from which to establish community contacts. In a recent survey, it was found that most group home residents had been in-patients for a prolonged period; one-third had spent over twenty years in hospital. Over half had been in the home for more than two years and three-quarters wanted to stay there. Staff thought that three-quarters had a lasting disability (slowness, under-activity, and social withdrawal being the chief problems) and would probably need sheltered accommodation permanently. It could not be said that residents were always 'integrated' into the community in the sense that we outlined at the beginning of this chapter. Many had no local friends, did not use local amenities, and remained in the community but not of it. Nevertheless, the opportunity for integration was there.

Residents of hostels, on the other hand, were more representative of people discharged from hospital after recent admissions. They were younger, more often men, with a shorter (though still substantial) history of hospital care. The diagnosis was less likely to be schizophrenia, more often neurosis or personality disorder, and behaviour was often more difficult and demanding. Staff thought that many would eventually leave for more independent accommodation.

There are long-stay hostels as well, particularly those run by the Mental After-Care Association, that provide sheltered living arrangements for more disabled people. Because of the living-in staff, hostels are much more expensive than group homes.

Another model for accommodation outside hospital is hotel or 'board and care' accommodation. Disabled people unable to work can use their social security money to pay for cheap accommodation such as has been provided commercially on a large scale in the United States. There have been criticisms that residents can be exploited by unscrupulous managers but also accounts of some schemes that are well-run and well-accepted by clients. A few excellent examples have been set up by charities in this country, with medical and social work consultation, but there is a general paucity of such accommodation.

Finally, there are a few sheltered communities in various parts of the country, set up by organisations such as Steiner. These have generally favourable reports but have not been independently evaluated. There is need for further experiments in this field.

Studies of people living in common lodging houses, Salvation Army hostels, government reception centres or sleeping rough have revealed (in this order) an increasing proportion of chronically mentally disabled people. Charitable organisations have shown that many such destitute people can be helped to live more settled lives, but the amount of decent accommodation available, particularly in the centre of large conurbations like London or Glasgow, is totally inadequate. The local authorities do not feel responsible since most of the 'vagrants' can be regarded as having 'no parish of origin', to quote a phrase from the days of the Poor Law. Central government grants do not begin to meet the need.[17]

Day care

Day hospitals are provided by District Health Authorities (about three-quarters of all day places); day centres by local authorities (about one-fifth) and voluntary organisations (5 per cent). Day hospitals are on a hospital site, in about three-quarters of instances. A survey of a national sample,[11] carried out in 1976, found a good deal of socio-demographic overlap in the clientele of the various types of centre, although the clinical measures used were not sufficiently discriminating to allow conclusions to be drawn. However, the severity of current symptoms (e.g. depression) is greater in day hospitals, which cater for acute conditions in about four-fifths of their clientele, than in day centres, half of whose users are chronically disabled. In other words, day hospitals treat many people who have the characteristics of short-stay in-patients. Some admissions to wards could be avoided if greater use were made of day hospitals. However, day hospitals also provide for some patients who could equally well be in day centres. There is no clear-cut division of function.

Over a third of day hospital patients and over half of day centre users had been attending for more than a year. Many other studies[27] have demonstrated this build-up of a long-stay clientele outside hospital. The staff of most day units describe their function as 'rehabilitative', but in fact clients are often more dependent than they need be because of a lack of facilities or encouragement for mutual support, useful occupations, domestic self-help (e.g. shopping, cooking and serving meals, managing a budget), using their own time constructively and participation in running the centre. The same is true of many hostels. The tendency to expect less and less of residents or day attenders as the years pass by is equivalent to the institutionalism that used to be characteristic of large mental hospitals. It can occur in the alternatives as well.

On the whole, day centres (like hostels and group homes) are tolerated by neighbours and, in some cases, actively welcomed. Some of the clientele may look a little odd or eccentric but they are mostly gentle people who do no harm and their right to live their lives, as they have to with their disabilities, is conceded. The *idea* of care outside hospital is a good one, but its realisation in practice is frequently unsatisfactory.

There has been no national survey of sheltered workshops, Industrial Therapy Organisations, etc., although these facilities are usually much appreciated. No doubt such a survey would reveal a shortage of places everywhere and a high proportion of districts with no provision at all.

It was admitted by the government spokesman in the Lords debate that only about half the number of places in non-hospital residential units, only about one-third of the day hospital places and only about a quarter of the places in local authority and voluntary day centres recommended in the Government White Paper of 1975[7] were actually available. There are parallel deficits in staffing ratios, particularly of nurses, occupational therapists and social workers experienced in the problems posed by mental illness, in the provision of hospital care near home, and in the time available for treatment and advice in out-patient clinics and general practitioners' surgeries.

Summary

When we consider the services and other forms of help actually provided for people afflicted by mental disorders, compared with the problems these people and their relatives face, we find large gaps and serious inadequacies. In contrast to a romantic vision of the help that will be forthcoming through informal community networks, people discharged from hospital are often socially isolated and unoccupied, and some are living in poverty or even destitution. They and their relatives are given little guidance, when disability becomes chronic, in how to 'live with mental illness'. Out-patient clinics are crowded, getting help in an emergency is often difficult, and the social services give psychiatric disorders a low priority. Residential and day care units are understaffed and places are in short supply. Coordination between the various services is often poor.

This is not what was envisaged when the run-down of the large hospitals began in the late 1950s. Although some people do receive a good service, and many recover in spite of one that is far from adequate, the overall picture, particularly for those with long-term disorders, is seriously unsatisfactory.

5 SIGNIFICANT INITIATIVES

Despite the severe shortfall of resources and lack of facilities within the community, several promising approaches are being pioneered by local authorities and voluntary agencies. During the course of our Enquiry we visited some of these and heard about others. It is not our intention to provide an inclusive list of such initiatives but to describe a selection of innovative projects to illustrate what can be done, often with very limited funds, to provide better services for the mentally ill.

One of the chief lessons to be derived from a study of the first four chapters is that help must begin at home. The stress involved when a member of the family is mentally ill, the demands made on other members of the family and the anxieties aroused among friends and neighbours must be of paramount concern. These stresses can lead to traumatic family crises if no support is available. The first example of a 'significant initiative' is a charity set up to provide such support.

The National Schizophrenia Fellowship

It was the recognition of this pressure on the family which led to the formation in 1972, of the National Schizophrenia Fellowship, a voluntary agency whose specific aim is to support the families of the mentally ill.[18]

It does this through the formation of local groups. Each group has a voluntary co-ordinator to organise regular meetings and events. The groups operate on the well-understood basis that nothing helps to break down the isolation and despair of individual families as much as to share their concern with others in a similar plight. At the same time, the groups try to increase understanding of schizophrenia and its attendant family problems among the general public, as well as among professional medical and social workers. With assistance and briefing from the NSF central office, groups have found ways of bringing their special problems home to Community Health Councils, Directors of Social Services, Chief Constables, Probation Officers, Marriage Guidance Councils, the Samaritans and other agencies who might find themselves involved with the mentally ill.

All the groups receive a quarterly Newsletter designed to relieve the sense of isolation that families feel when confronted with the stress and personal experience of mental illness. Some groups have now become large enough to be self-supporting within the overall national framework. This development is occurring in Scotland, the North-West, the North and Northern Ireland, and is being encouraged elsewhere.

A community psychiatric nursing scheme

Self-help groups are an important form of support, but they need ready access to services if they are to be practicable. One of the professional elements that can bridge the present gulf between community needs and services is the community psychiatric nursing service. Patients and relatives speak highly of the care they give. Community Psychiatric Nurses not only offer an important support for those coming out of hospital, but also help to prevent admissions. Although the service began in the late fifties it is at present under-valued and we feel should be developed beyond the present sparse provision of about 1 to 40,000 in England and Wales.

It is notable, for instance, that out of an establishment of 560 nursing staff attached to hospitals in the Basingstoke area, only 17 work in people's homes, in day centres or some other extramural resource. Nevertheless, even this small group of Community Psychiatric Nurses were maintaining some 600 people in the community through their efforts, about one-third of whom would otherwise have had to be admitted to hospital for want of professional support. Hospitals should use more of their nursing staff in this preventive and supporting role in the community, working with psychiatric social workers and general practitioners as well as psychiatrists. Indeed, the North Camden community psychiatric nursing service[6] has demonstrated the value of Community Psychiatric Nurses working as part of the primary care team, allocated to general practices everywhere. Such moves would, of course, require special training of the nursing staff, and it points to an area where a move towards 'community care' has important and direct implications for hospital staffing.

One important feature of the work of the Basingstoke Community Psychiatric Nurses is a twenty-four hour telephone service which enables families under stress to obtain advice quickly. Within the large Basingstoke area the aim—unless immediate intervention is needed—is to make an initial visit within forty-eight hours of being informed through this telephone link, or through some other channel of referral. Following the initial assessment by the Community Psychiatric Nurse, it is then quite usual for a case conference to be called, or for the nursing staff to seek more specialised help. Where there is close collaboration between the services and co-ordination of resources, this can result in the public receiving prompt, expert and sympathetic help at the point of need.

Craigmillar day centre

An attempt to offer a mix of professional and voluntary support within a community setting is at the heart of the Craigmillar Day Centre project in Edinburgh. This experimental scheme, set in a deprived housing estate of some 27,000 inhabitants suffering high unemployment and severe social problems is housed in a flat, open six days a week. The flat itself is rented by a local community group called the Craigmillar Festival Society which administers salaries and manages the services.

Among the novel features of this project is the active involvement of the community psychiatrist, formally attached to the Royal Edinburgh Hospital, who is finding new ways of interacting with the community, as well as with statutory and voluntary agencies. Self-referrals and informal referrals from all the primary care agencies, such as doctors, health visitors, social workers, community workers and the clergy are encouraged, and many of them accompany their own clients on a first visit. The community psychiatric nurse, equally, uses the facility to introduce his/her patients to such a resource.

The scheme has an organiser and a professional counsellor, supported by a local group of professional and community workers. This group provides a wide range of support for those using the centre; including a free meal (cooked by the users themselves), social encounters and a range of arts and crafts projects, counselling, home visits by the counsellor, group meetings, informal and more regular contact with the community psychiatrist and referral to other psychiatric services if necessary.

About a third of those using the centre have alcohol-related problems. Another third are ex-psychiatric patients and the remainder suffer from social or personality problems. Those using the centre, mainly women, range in age from 20 to 65 years. In the first nine months of the scheme, 92 new clients visited the centre at least once, with 34 using it regularly and 15 attending on a daily basis. Yet the cost of this project (£5,000 for salaries and £3,000 for rent, fuel and subsistence) is extremely modest, and is subsidised by voluntary effort from within the community, raising money for additional activities. The users of this scheme are offered a wide range of services in an informal non-institutional setting, and, at the same time, are encouraged to improve their self-help and coping *abilities*, particularly if they are ex-psychiatric patients. The project also offers an informal setting for multi-disciplinary professional practice, and it is this feature which differentiates it from the more standard form of day centre, and which offers the prospect of new ways of working with the mentally ill.

As the Community Psychiatrist herself has written about the scheme: 'The medical qualifications and autonomy of the community psychiatrist may help to provide more "authority" for initiating new contacts and offering consultation services, etc., although the medical and psychiatric training of the psychiatrist is possibly no more appropriate for such work than a social science qualification.'

Eastgate House

Another attempt to provide both flexible day centre facilities and a focus for inter-disciplinary practice opened in Lewes, East Sussex, in 1979, at Eastgate House. Established through joint financing in a building in the centre of the town, Eastgate House carried further the idea of professionals working together within the community, and outside their own institutional bases. Apart from a co-ordinator, the centre is staffed on a rota basis by a psychiatrist, psychologist, community psychiatric nurse, social worker and occupational therapist, each working there from half a day to two days per week. In this role they act as 'duty officers', seeing clients, linking with other services, offering professional guidance and working with volunteers from the community who help man the telephones and welcome callers. This close link between volunteers from the community and professional workers is promising and adds to the variety of skills which such a local resource can gather together in an informal way.

Volunteers, however, need support. One of the problems that the Eastgate project has encountered is that volunteers cannot easily provide a constant, full-time service. Equally, while multi-disciplinary interaction is admirable, it will not work if the professional staff are constantly changing, so that long-term relationships cannot be built up and the entire burden of cohesion is placed on the co-ordinator. A stable staff is an essential ingredient of such a project.

Nevertheless, Eastgate House does provide a model for flexible, accessible and responsible day care. It has developed an impressive range of activities in a weekly programme that is flexible enough to use available local skills or meet known local needs. There are self-help groups, a group for people with phobic fears, a support group for manic depressives and their relatives, a bereavement group, and activities such as a lunch group, etc., relaxation classes, meetings with single parents and their children, and some drama and self-expression sessions. The centre is also the meeting place for the community-based self-help group for alcohol abuse, and it could become the focus of other related community needs and interests. In particular, it has developed a referral system for crisis work, through the duty office, in which the community can be linked to a variety of appropriate services at the point of need. Through its network of volunteers, such a crisis service may well be developed to offer appropriate help to families or individuals trying to cope with mental illness in their own homes.

A 'drop-in' centre

Eastgate House is essentially a centre for those who have already identified their needs or had them identified by others. Within the wider community, however, there is equally a need for more open-ended 'drop-in' centres which do not seek to provide a particular service, but which act largely as a social facility, while at the same time having access to more specific services. There are many forms of 'drop-in' centres, often run by voluntary agencies. One example, for the young, often homeless and rootless people coming into a metropolis like London, is situated just off the West End. It operates an open-door policy and acts as a club, a contact point, an information centre and a meeting place for the dispossessed. There are good contacts with professional agencies, particularly with community psychiatric nurses and with health visitors, psychiatric social workers and general practitioners. Such a centre can provide informal comfort and support and act as a link in the chain of multi-disciplinary primary care. By operating within the community, and joining up the statutory services in a way that is often difficult to achieve from within the professions themselves, such an agency can effectively match the real needs of individuals with the most appropriate forms of service, combined with community support. It is an excellent example of voluntary effort.

The Richmond Fellowship

'Drop-in' centres can form the first point of contact with appropriate services for those rendered vulnerable by mental distress. For many, however, the ability to cope with such disturbance on their own or within their own family setting is simply not possible. Too many find themselves hospitalised when their real needs can be better met within the community. A voluntary agency like the Richmond Fellowship, which operates more than forty therapeutic communities[15] throughout the United Kingdom, offers a radical alternative within the community setting. The Fellowship, founded in 1959 as a direct response to the debates that led to the Mental Health Act of that year, works with a wide range of emotionally disturbed and mentally ill people. Schizophrenics, the depressed, recovering alcoholics, drug abusers, emotionally unstable adolescents and children, families requiring a period of intensive support are all housed by the Fellowship, at a cost to society which is well below the level of institutional care. More important than cost, however, is the fact that such therapeutic communities are rehabilitative in their aims and practice.

Overall, the average length of stay of an adult resident within the Fellowship is between nine months and a year, at the end of which time the majority either move to independent living or, at times, to more sheltered accommodation in group homes or to community residences, where a good deal of discreet support is available, but where residents can lead maximally independent lives on a semi-permanent basis—usually without otherwise unavoidable intermittent hospitalisation.

Residential community care at the time of the Mental Health Act of 1959 was on the whole visualised as a physical move of patients and their carers from large institutions away from the community to smaller buildings within the community, but little thought had been given to the possibility that the carers might need a very different orientation, and that the motivation of staff to accept a specific role might not suit them equally for a different one. Although concepts of the therapeutic community had been developed in a number of hospitals, with an increased appreciation of the need of individuals to be helped to determine their own life and to contribute to the well-being of others by word and action, the extent to which this could be realised was limited by the size of the institution and by traditional roles and boundaries.

The 1959 Act gave a natural stimulus to the possibility of experimentation and to an approach which would maximise the normal life situation for residents, to test out in ordinary settings the extent to which they could accept responsibility and respond positively to the invitation to give assistance, rather than just be a recipient, and to change in response to individual and joint exploration of their specific problems. The idea of a therapeutic community outside the hospital, without medical supervision other than that available to out-patients generally, was at first an anathema to many, and the Fellowship was more than once in danger of having to give up. However, the speed at which it has grown and become professionally accepted points to the need for its specific contribution.

The approach of the Fellowship to the mentally ill discourages the attitude that they are 'patients' and dependent; it adopts the view that they are potentially capable individuals afflicted with problems, many of which are temporary and can be overcome, at least to a large extent, with the help of the group as well as the community outside. The mentally ill are treated as potentially independent persons, capable of running their own lives, making decisions about their futures and bearing responsibility for their own actions. The therapeutic community aims to maximise the residents' capacity for autonomy and to enhance relationships by widening understanding of self and others, and by appealing to the stronger aspects of their life and personality. Within a Richmond Fellowship community, the residents, largely referred by psychiatrists of all schools, but also directed there by social workers and by a wide range of other agencies, take part in a variety of group experiences and activities, as well as receiving personal counselling and other individual attention. They share in activities designed to develop life skills, such as cooking and home decorating, role playing to help them obtain jobs or improve relationships, and discussions about attitudes, world affairs and spiritual values. Medication, if relevant, is carefully controlled under the supervision of their own general practitioner or psychiatrist. Links with families are fostered and each community actively interacts with its own locality. Some residents find part-time, others full-time, employment in the neighbourhood. Others do voluntary work or help to run the House and prepare for work outside through the in-house work training which focuses on the development of skills, work attitudes and relationships as well as the furthering of personal talents and meeting the needs of a household or a community.

The task of activating a therapeutic community of this type is undertaken by staff who are not only carefully recruited for the work, but are trained to do so by the Fellowship itself. The need for skilled and perceptive staff in working with the mentally ill is an issue that we discuss in greater detail in Chapter 8. It is relevant to stress here, however, that the issue of suitably qualified staff is critical to the community resources we advocate. Medical or social work training, while obviously relevant, is not in itself sufficient to prepare staff for rehabilitative and therapeutic functions. Nor are suitable training courses widely available. The skills and experience required are complex, the knowledge base wide and the theoretical framework diverse.

Hence the Fellowship has pioneered not only the concept of a therapeutic community outside the hospital—which is now widely accepted —but its own training programmes, by drawing on its own experience as well as that of other organisations. These programmes are recognised as unique and valuable, not only for staff in therapeutic communities but also for other members of the caring professions whose work requires a sound understanding of individual and group behaviour and problems. This role of pioneering new forms of care, and of developing the necessary experience, training and infra-structure for them, is an essential feature of the voluntary sector, which will be more fully discussed in Chapter 6.

In many cases, after a form of service has been shown to be effective, it can be left to statutory bodies to select the models or ingredients considered useful, and then to apply them on a wider scale. In the case of the Fellowship, local authorities and other government departments, including colleges, have adopted therapeutic community models, especially in relation to the use of peer groups for residents, as well as group work training for staff. Often this has come about most readily by recruiting staff who have undergone the Fellowship's two-year training programme.

Nevertheless, the organisation has functions which cannot easily be replicated by local government. The Fellowship's diversity of services—providing a continuum of care—combined with its training programme, creates not only a large element of choice and of appropriate help for the consumer, but also provides interesting and rewarding career structures for staff, thus giving a proper value to a social work role that is often under-valued, and attracting recruits of a high calibre. The variety of client groups, the content of, and the contact in, training and consultative work with the staff, and the different viewpoints and different cultures represented among the staff make for an exciting and challenging work environment.

The staff in the Fellowship's communities are in a particularly favourable position to further the integration which community care exists to promote. The traditional avoidance of encounter with mental illness has led to unnecessarily prolonged periods in hospital or to isolation within the community. The halfway houses not only function as a bridge for residents on their way to independent living. They are also a safe place where members of the wider community can come to terms with their fears and prejudices in relation to ex-mental patients and where they can learn—in relation to their own life and conduct perhaps—how to counter factors which lead to breakdown. Both in a national and international context, staff have found that the joint development of expertise and of a strategy for action can overcome resistance and bring about understanding, acceptance and integration.

Portugal Prints

Apart from the need for residential care in a community setting, an important element in a network of caring services for the mentally ill is the 'rehabilitation workshop', providing an economic status that many of them need and offering care and guidance in the acquisition of new, marketable skills. Portugal Prints, a workshop set up by the Westminster Association for Mental Health, with a budget of £40,000 and operating from a series of basement rooms in central London, is one example of such a venture.

With a permanent staff of three, its aim is to provide a therapeutic environment created through the discipline and satisfaction of collective work, as well as moving towards rehabilitation and employment in the outside world. To achieve this, the project had to find an attractive end-product, which was labour-intensive and needing a variety of skills, but which was also manageable within a confined space. The product should not be so complicated that workers could not relate to all stages of its manufacture, but should provide them with the opportunity to move from one process to another. The solution, after various experiments, was to produce 'up-market' paintings and designs on metal which, when polished and trimmed, lead to a variety of products such as boxes, mirrors, key fobs, luggage labels and prints.

On most days anything up to twenty people arrive at Portugal Prints for work. They operate in the administrative section, on the industrial processes of transferring designs from templates on to metal, on polishing and trimming metal sheets, on mounting these, and on packing and despatch. The workers are not paid a wage, but are provided with bus fares, free coffee and tea, and a weekly stipend of about two pounds. Their involvement is not seen as 'work' but as 'a means towards re-habilitation' since the aim of the scheme is to re-discover how to concentrate on a task, how to be punctual, to work within a group, and to find commitment to a job and good interpersonal relationships, all of which are impaired by mental illness.

Portugal Prints does not offer occupational therapy or sheltered work for chronically disabled people for whom a day centre project, one of the long-term therapeutic communities within the Richmond Fellowship, or a Remploy factory might be more appropriate. Rather, it caters for a much smaller group of those who are genuinely able to move towards complete recuperation and full-time or part-time commercial employment. The experience of working within an industrial environment which matches its output to the pace and needs of its work force rather than the demands of commerce is a necessary component in any comprehensive network of recovery facilities for the mentally ill. Very few such opportunities exist at present, and those available are often forced to be concerned more with their economic viability than with being therapeutically effective. We earnestly advocate an extension of provision offering rehabilitative work experience for the mentally ill.

Summary

Some of the significant initiatives that have emerged in recent years, which could, with advantage, be incorporated into a comprehensive community mental health service, have been described. We could have cited many others. (See references 14, 15, 18, 22, 27, 29.) Each district requires a network of provision including a 'drop-in' centre, day centres, multi-disciplinary professional teams, a variety of forms of residential care and sheltered work experience, as well as a co-ordinated communication system which will offer families the opportunity to obtain an appropriate pattern of services. The voluntary sector has a particularly creative role to play in providing these facilities, which has been under-valued and under-utilised by the statutory system. We consider this role in Chapter 6.

6 THE ROLE OF THE VOLUNTARY SECTOR

In the United Kingdom the voluntary sector, which includes non-government charitable organisations concerned with the welfare of individuals and families, has always played an important role, by no means diminished by the development of the 'welfare state'. Recent reports, from the Wolfenden Committee on *The Future of Voluntary Organisations*,[30] and the *Barclay Committee on Social Workers—Their Role and Tasks*,[1] have underlined the necessity for a strong voluntary sector, and the Department of Health and Social Security, in a Consultative Document on community care,[10] also emphasised that 'the voluntary organisations play an indispensable part in our society'.

Four main functions of the voluntary sector

The Wolfenden Committee identified four main areas where the voluntary sector plays a major role. The first is initiating new work in areas where a need is apparent but no government action has been taken. In the sphere of support and counselling for families, the Family Service Units and the Family Welfare Association spring to mind, and, in the field of drug addiction, Phoenix House. The new, the difficult, the contentious or the speculative approach has often been undertaken by voluntary organisations. Second, the voluntary sector may provide a complementary, additional or alternative service to that provided by statutory bodies, allowing some element of choice. Mencap (Royal Society for Mentally Handicapped Children and Adults), the Marriage Guidance Council and Help the Aged are examples. Third, voluntary bodies often act as pressure groups. Such agencies as MIND[2] (National Association for Mental Health), Shelter and the Child Poverty Action Group have chivvied the statutory authorities and offered advocacy services on behalf of the poor. (A new move into more active and outspoken campaigning has often been marked by a change of name and image—the National Old People's Welfare Council, for instance, became Age Concern, and the National Association for Mental Health is now known as MIND.) Fourth, the Wolfenden Committee recognised that a voluntary agency may be the sole provider of a service: it may fill a need that would otherwise go unmet, such as the plight of battered women, now recognised by the provision of refuges. A most important function, not sufficiently considered by Wolfenden, is that

45

of representation by the consumers themselves—the patients and their families—such as the National Schizophrenia Fellowship.[2]

In the field of mental health, voluntary agencies play every one of these roles. While they do not have, or claim, a monopoly of innovation, some of the examples illustrated in Chapter 5 indicated that they often provide services which are both new and which operate in areas unserved by the statutory sector. In terms of numbers, the voluntary sector almost matches the local authority contribution in the provision of residential care for the mentally ill in the community. In 1979, in England, seven-eighths of all beds for the mentally ill were provided in NHS hospitals. About a quarter of the small-scale 'community' provision was in voluntary homes and hostels.

Overall, the voluntary sector provides about one-fifth of all the homes and hostels available to the mentally ill in the community in England and Wales. When account is taken of the quality of the provision in terms, for instance, of the availability of trained staff, the contribution of the voluntary sector is much greater. Overall figures, in any case, mask the reliance which many local authorities place on voluntary agencies. Among the London boroughs, for example, the voluntary sectors were, in 1980, providing 62 per cent of all the residential care requirements of the Inner Boroughs, and 38 per cent of the needs of the Outer Boroughs. As the detailed breakdown also indicates, however, there were individual London boroughs where these proportions were much higher. In the case of therapeutic communities outside the hospital, run by specially trained staff, a voluntary agency, the Richmond Fellowship, is practically the sole provider on a national scale.

The fact that in recent decades the voluntary societies have thrived, sought new approaches and taken on tough challenges has been widely and publicly acknowledged. In some areas, such as care for the blind, the mentally handicapped and the elderly, the contribution of non-statutory organisations is so large that the State could not cope without them. Altogether, the voluntary sector constitutes a significant slice of the total welfare system, employing, at the latest count, some 1,700 field-workers and 20,000 residential and day-care staff. In 1975–6, the income of 65 national voluntary organisations equalled 10 per cent of the total expenditure of local authorities' social service departments.

Minimal standards ignored

In the face of this level of contribution, it is to be expected that Governments should continue to express support for the voluntary sector; nevertheless, the track record of successive governments in power gives rise to unease. Certainly, in the sphere of community care for the adult mentally ill, they have so far failed to meet their own minimal standards, and appear to be content to continue to do so. The White Paper, 'Better Services for the Mentally Ill',[7] laid down planning guidelines for integrated district services, but these guidelines were qualified both in the body of the White Paper and in the foreword contributed by the then Secretary of State for Social Services, by the warning that financial constraints made this only a general and long-term goal.

Moreover, the current climate seems to give even more cause for alarm. The positive utterances on the contribution of the voluntary organisations, made by the present Government before taking office were disquieting. In January, 1981, at the conference held at Swanwick on the Voluntary Services Unit, Sir George Young (then Parliamentary Under Secretary, Department of Health and Social Security) said: 'I have no doubt that the time is ripe for developing local voluntary action; people are more aware than they have been for a generation that there are and should be limits to what the government will provide.' He went on to make the unrealistic suggestion that if 'the people themselves' care, they will provide not only services but funds to run the services, without relying on monies derived from taxes or rates. Such statements confirm the impression that Government support for the voluntary sector stems from financial expediency, rather than from the only valid basis for support: to provide the most comprehensive network of services to meet client need on the basis of value for money. It may therefore be useful to summarise the benefits of the voluntary sector and to examine the criticisms.

Commitment of voluntary staff

A major asset of voluntary organisations is that, in spite of an increasing professionalism they can engender and maintain a high level of commitment from workers, which generally benefits the immediate client group and which also permeates and influences the field as a whole. The voluntary agency's ability to recruit staff with more than usual commitment may be thought to deprive the statutory services, but the natural interchange of staff between the voluntary and statutory sectors is likely to redress the balance. It may be held that commitment is a relative value, that staff need a shorter working week to gain refreshment and distance from their clients in order to give of their best, and that 'self-giving' is not always healthily based. Nevertheless, the voluntary sector guards the values of solidarity with one's fellow men and of that self-giving which is basically not neurotic or sentimental but acknowledges the true value of one's brother or neighbour.

Another strength of the voluntary agency, especially pertinent in the field of mental health, is its ability to involve the local community. An important problem of adult mentally ill people is isolation and estrangement from society. Means need to be devised whereby both sides can overcome unease, fear, prejudice and separation, and where genuine integration can take place. Such a process does not readily take place in a government-run service; not only does bureaucracy tend to interfere with spontaneity and informal 'human relationships' but the fact that a service is government-run might make the neighbourhood less willing to contribute personally. By contrast, because relatively independent of government, the voluntary agency is more dependent on the immediate neighbourhood and society at large. The reliance of the organisation on neighbourhood support makes for close involvement and allows the voluntary agency to exploit its unique strengths. It is usually anticipated, for example, that a new facility for the mentally ill will be resisted by the local community, yet neighbourhoods respond very positively when they have been carefully canvassed before a halfway house is set up in their midst. Instead of receiving a formal notice which gives information on how to object to planning permission, neighbours are visited by staff and by residents. The latter especially are in a unique position to explain the project and their need for it, with the usual result of a warm welcome being extended. MIND and Mencap are examples of organisations which both rely on and support their local membership in such projects as the provision of group homes, sheltered facilities, clubs and fund-raising enterprises, such as charity shops. The public is often portrayed as indifferent and selfish, but when appealed to directly they usually rise to the occasion. A voluntary organisation has, therefore, a distinct advantage in its ability to address and successfully appeal to the imagination and sympathy of ordinary people; as a result a halfway house can truly become part of the neighbourhood and community, and integration can take place.

Provision for training

Another significant area in which the voluntary sector generally has led the field is that of the provision of training—especially for residential work. The Barclay Report recognised the low standard of training among staff in the statutory sector of residential care. It pointed out that 80 per cent of residential staff have received no *relevant* training, and supplied the following statement from the Residential Care Association, emphasising the conflict between *staff* needs and *client* needs: 'The current patterns of training and promotion are in direct conflict with clients' wishes for continuity of professional contact and residents suffer seriously in some establishments because of high staff turnover.'

It is therefore not only an increased quantity of trained staff that is needed, but an increase in quality. This is especially true in certain specialist fields, and here the Barclay Report recognised the advantages of the voluntary sector. Expertise requires a body of experience which is based on a philosophy and systematic thinking and work, including a code of ethics. The statutory services recruit staff from generic social work courses which rarely provide the skills relevant to specialist residential care. The large voluntary organisation is able to tailor its training to a specific philosophy and defined standards. It can provide on an ongoing basis opportunities for further development, through staff contact, consultation and joint learning. The role of training cannot be over-estimated since within that framework people can explore differences and come to a genuine understanding of people and of the degree of consensus needed to work together flexibly and effectively.

Staff of residential services are in an unusually powerful position to create either a positive or negative environment for those in their care. They therefore have particular need of training which helps them to understand human conduct generally, and particularly the conflicts and anxieties which govern the behaviour of the residents; they need to intervene in a manner which enhances the residents' awareness and acceptance of themselves and others, and helps them to make changes in the direction of greater autonomy. At the same time staff should be in a position to appreciate societal expectations and to help the residents to gain the rewards of meeting the challenge and achieving integration. In this respect the preparation of staff to bring about a fruitful encounter between the mentally ill and 'normal' people is more easily undertaken by the voluntary organisation than by the official social work training schemes. A specially designed training programme helps staff to address the heart of the problem: how can those who are disadvantaged through emotional disturbance or mental illness be enabled to form a proper and valued part of an integrated society? How can residential and day care be provided in a way that enhances the dignity, skills, and sense of responsibility and fulfilment in the residents?

Developing specialisms

Another important value which many voluntary organisations can supply is their specialism. Whilst in most local government positions social workers have to deal with a large variety of needs and Social Services Departments can only hope to cater minimally for a wide client group, the voluntary sector can specialise in its own field and create within it a number of services which are more sensitive to the needs of individuals. The experience gathered overall within such an organisation is greater than a local authority can hope to gather, or constantly to draw on. Nor is it reasonable to expect the authority to create a complete range of facilities which a 'continuum of care' would require if the client population cannot warrant this. Whilst some joint ventures of local authorities can establish specialist work or a common approach to certain problems in the field of mental health, it is usually more advantageous to local authorities to draw on services provided by specialist voluntary organisations. The fact that residents can move according to their need, through services that are connected and based on an identical philosophy and common practice, is of major benefit in providing the appropriate degree of support. The maintenance of a social network operative within the organisation is also important.

As has been stated, Government enthusiasm for voluntary effort often fails at the point where material aid is needed, and in justification the voluntary organisation may be accused of 'lack of accountability'. The DHSS Consultative Document, 'The Government and the Voluntary Sector',[9] purported to make a favourable comment when it stated that 'where the Government chooses to spend its money to support the work of a voluntary body, it is deliberately choosing a system which is independent of a direct control'. However, the Barclay Report found that 'a common reason given for not allowing a voluntary agency a greater say or share in planning and providing social services was that it was perceived as not being accountable in the same way as a local authority'.

This is a complex area; it is not always clear to whom the voluntary agency is accountable. The Health Authorities and Social Services Department have a clear accountability to the tax and rate payers, which may result in a conservative and unimaginative service. Accountability in a specialist agency is to a more enlightened and involved body of supporters, including those local authorities which regularly use its services, and therefore a more radical programme can be carried through. Furthermore, in times of recession, a voluntary agency's commitment to a particular cause may enable it to continue with a specific programme whilst local and central government provisions are being cut back or closed down as economy measures. However, where voluntary agencies depend heavily on government funding, this may be cut (in order to pacify the rate payer), in favour of government services which may be more costly and less effective.

In the above mentioned document, 'The Government and the Voluntary Sector', the foreword states that the public at large and private donors can rightly expect to know, in the case of organisations which receive central or local authority grants, what has been achieved with the money provided out of their taxes, rates and gifts. There is a growing body of opinion among voluntary organisations themselves that more care should be devoted to monitoring their own performance, in the interests of providing a better service to their clients and ensuring that the highest professional standards are maintained. A more standardised system of accounting, such as is now required in the US, may serve the purpose of providing greater opportunity for assessing the comparative contribution of the voluntary organisations, but more research is needed as well, comparing the various approaches of statutory and voluntary organisations. However, funding for such projects is not readily available.

Ability to be selective

The other major reservation about the voluntary organisation is that it is able to be selective in its area of work and in its target group—which can lead to elitism. Indeed, this very charge was made in September, 1982, by the Shadow Minister for Social Services (Conference of Association of Directors of Social Services in Hertford). Linked to this is obviously the concept of universal provision available to all on an equal basis regardless of social standing or ability to pay. However, although the target group of a voluntary organisation may be circumscribed, the majority of beneficiaries are socially deprived and, in spite of statutory provision, are not appropriately cared for.

It is in this context that it may be appropriate to mention the extent to which clients experience and/or express dissatisfaction with existing local authority services. For example, whilst elitism should be avoided, there is a proper place for ensuring that those who have been deprived by circumstance of illness or emotional distress, are not further deprived of obvious needs, such as congenial fellow members in a half way house or group home with whom common interests can be pursued. The same goes for day centres and sheltered training facilities. Especially the day care unit, whilst generally considered essential to 'occupy people and relieve the family', is often found futile, depressing, uncongenial and boring. Group homes, whilst providing a commonsense and most economic option for people who should not live alone, can also be an inappropriate option, as can return to the family of origin. Unless within the immediate group the resources for mutual support can be generated, the individuals concerned are at one another's mercy. The cheap option becomes then a *cover-up for lack of care*.

How support should be offered

It has been argued above that the voluntary organisation is in a strong position to deliver community mental health services. There are compelling reasons for central and local government assistance to voluntary bodies on an adequate and sustained basis—but how is this assistance to be delivered? In the field of mental health, in particular, there has so far been a tendency to continue to provide resources through the existing power-structures, such as the health services. Adequate provision outside hospital, on a continuum from crisis intervention to long-term provision, has not been made. In view of the high proportion of the population who at one time or another will need help for mental ill-health (Chapter 3), the concentration of care within the clinical system is an obvious imbalance, and can create an unnecessary stigma for people for whom other forms of help would be appropriate.

Easy access must be available to medical services for people at risk, but many other community services must be provided, since the concept of community care involves promotion of the highest possible participation in 'normal life'. It is also essential that the staff concerned understand the complex psychological issues involved.

The lack of progress made to realise the radical moves from institutional care to community care which were proposed in the 1959 Mental Health Act points to resistance and reservations which exist not only in the community, but also in the health service. An obvious reason for resistance to the diminished use of institutional and clinical settings is the threat both to job security and satisfaction and to the status of the staff.

With the transition from in-patient to community care the question of re-deployment of staff naturally arises. Apart from the increasing need for community psychiatric nurses (for which there is careful selection), a number of nurses and other hospital staff—previously employed by the hospital—will be needed for facilities in the community where their specific expertise is essential; others will need retraining in order to cope with new roles and acquire a new orientation. The voluntary sector, if given a brief, could take a major part in the retraining of those who look for a role in community care, not only in a social but in a medical setting.

The challenge to both central and local government, having professed its support for the voluntary sector, is to ensure that finance is made directly available and to create new patterns of joint planning which do not stem from pre-conceived and tradition-bound structures. In the new planning machinery the voluntary sector needs to have an equitable share in the decision-making, especially where expertise can be made widely available; however, the Government has so far not conceded this.

Joint financing and planning by Consultative Committees of the mid-seventies—designed as a major step in the direction of improved and comprehensive services filling a gap—has generally been recognised to be concerned more with supplementing under-financed services than as a measure towards better provision for needs of the community. In a parliamentary answer of July 28, 1982, the Secretary of State for Social Services said that 'district health authorities will in future be able to guarantee continuing annual payments to local authorities and voluntary organisations for people moving into community care'. How adequate the payments, how appropriate the criteria of transfer, and how much affected other groups in need, remains to be seen. In the absence of a strong legislative mandate, and a strong co-ordinating and funding agent, the stance taken by local government becomes all-important.

Policies need direction

Voluntary organisations are bound to be affected by the priorities set by local government. Much distress has been caused when local authorities have made economies by cutting back on their sponsorship of applicants for voluntary care. Some local authorities use a quota system—one out, one in—either for a specific kind of service such as a hostel, or for a specific organisation. Other authorities, in practice, have turned away from using any aftercare whatsoever since the area of mental health appears to be the easiest on which to make cuts. Others again, fearing reproach from the taxpayer, utilise exclusively their own under-used services, whether or not these meet the need of the person concerned. But even where local authorities have agreed to meet the total operational costs of residential care in a voluntary organisation, problems are encountered. For example, fees for the Richmond Fellowship's houses were initially calculated on an occupancy rate of 85 per cent, which was satisfactory for a number of years. In the lean years, however, it transpired that many authorities failed to make the necessary resources available to take up that level of occupancy so that, in effect, a considerable shortfall of income ensued. The conclusions to be drawn from such inefficient deployment of resources must be that, *unless local authorities combine to set a direction for their policies, they will not make the best use of facilities which are available to them on a per capita cost basis.* If (for the sake of argument) 100 per cent use of urgently needed facilities costs the local authority only 5 per cent more than 75 per cent use, then it is folly for local authorities not to take up all places. Such 'folly', however, may simply be the effect of separate decision-making in separate administrative areas, each of which values its autonomy more than a commonly determined use of funds—'buying less' for the same investment.

'Buying more' is bound to result in an association with the market place and with contracts for services. Nevertheless, even the DHSS contracts for consultancy services, for example from universities. But contracts for client services, in this case for the mentally ill or emotionally disturbed, have not been looked on with favour in Great Britain, and admittedly not without reason. If we look to the United States as 'the market place' *par excellence*, we see a government awarding contracts to those who are seeking profit as against those who wish to provide human services. Any new area of funding is likely to be depleted quickly by agencies which (being profit-making and therefore having funds at their disposal to act) are able to cash in on new government deals. When the government changes its focus to a different field, such agencies change their focus accordingly and the end result is plundered government coffers, and a population in need. Such an example should not, however, deter our government from awarding direct contracts to national organisations which can provide services across the country efficiently, sensitively and economically, and whose track record demonstrates practice and commitment of a high standard.

It is important, however, to avoid certain pitfalls which beset service contracts and bid systems in the United States, and which by no means are confined to the profit-making sector. Wheeling and dealing is one very unsatisfactory aspect of purchase of service arrangements. In addition, the system encourages bidders to promise services which are not, or cannot be maintained, at a proper level. Bureaucratic requirements abound, but once these are satisfied, monitoring is poor. The amount of energy that is wasted by many organisations seeking to compete for limited resources is enormous. Contracts should be awarded more on the basis of proven ability of an organisation than by a superficial look at savings.

The need for direct funding

A community service must rely on regular and adequate statutory income to function. Charitably-minded individuals, industries and foundations cannot be expected to provide both the capital *and* the operating costs of essential services needed by the public. In the case of mental health endeavours, there is a strong connection between emotional attitudes of the public and financial constraints imposed upon voluntary organisations. Some client groups attract more voluntary and government funds than others. A survey undertaken by Judith Unell[5, 25] demonstrates that the mentally ill have not attracted a strong lobby, and the attitude of society towards mental illness is an added burden with which voluntary bodies especially have to cope. Government has the benefit of a substantial subsidy in terms of capital costs being provided through voluntary giving and receives a further benefit by the fact that operating costs in voluntary organisations are usually considerably less than services run directly by government. As a former Secretary of State for Health and Social Services said: 'This whole field is one in which the local authorities should make the fullest use of voluntary bodies; pound for pound, they are a better buy.'

It is acknowledged that Social Services Departments are themselves grievously starved of resources. Neither the local authorities nor the voluntary organisations should have to engage in a battle for resources, with the resulting waste of energy. Nor should the voluntary organisation have to engage in multiple approaches to multiple agencies, which fail to combine effectively, although each of them has some power. Instead, there should be an opportunity for the voluntary organisation to submit a circumscribed plan which it is capable of implementing and of which local authorities can avail themselves. The funding for such a plan should come from the DHSS direct and should be geared towards creating essential facilities where these do not already exist. The present cutbacks, against which the voluntary organisation is even more defenceless than the statutory sector, could lead to dismantled services which would take years and high costs to rebuild. This country cannot afford such wastage, nor even a standstill. There is an urgent need for speeding up the provision of facilities in the community to close the ever-widening gap of non-provision. The government should by direct contract use the potential of the voluntary organisations, which can move flexibly and fast, provide services sensitively and economically at the point of need, and train and mobilise forces substantially in a comparatively short period.

Summary

The contribution of the voluntary sector is no less vital now than in the era before the Welfare State, although the role of the voluntary sector has undergone a process of change and adaptation. The Wolfenden Committee Report identified four major ways in which voluntary organisations make their contribution. Some client-groups, for example the blind, mentally handicapped and elderly, could not receive a viable service through statutory provision alone; other groups, such as the emotionally disturbed, would be deprived of adequate and appropriate services.

Successive governments have acknowledged the necessity for the voluntary sector but the extent of government support has shown considerable ambivalence. Recent statements give particular cause for concern by implying that the voluntary sector may be expected to replace rather than complement statutory services and may be starved of government funding simultaneously.

The voluntary sector has several strengths. Staff idealism and commitment are high, and can help to keep welfare services aware of the need to be 'client-orientated'. The public are willing to become involved in helping voluntary organisations, thus assisting the integration with the local community and promoting community education and prevention. Specialist voluntary organisations lead the way in staff training, especially in residential work.

The voluntary organisation can offer a wide range and depth of provision: a nation-wide network of specialist services in any given field is more efficient than the fragmented and incomplete facilities which one local authority is capable of providing.

Voluntary services are sometimes accused of lack of accountability. It is true that voluntary organisations need to improve their monitoring procedures and to standardise their accounting. However, most voluntary organisations are accountable to a responsible body of supporters, many of them closely involved with the relevant client-group and therefore committed to scrutinising the organisation's policy and practice. Another criticism is that voluntary organisations are selective. However, this carries the advantage of specialisation and the expertise gained is not only valuable to clients whose needs are not otherwise met, but also leads to improvement in statutory practice.

The attempt to provide comprehensive community care for those afflicted with mental disorders of all degrees of severity requires a shift in resources towards statutory and voluntary services based locally. This will require schemes to enable the staff of the large hospitals to be redeployed and retrained.

Voluntary organisations are accustomed to responding promptly to need and to operating efficiently on minimum incomes. The Department of Health and local authorities should combine to support the voluntary sector and exploit its skills to the full. Experience in the United States has demonstrated a number of ways in which contracts to specialised agencies can be misused but this experience also shows how the disadvantages can be avoided. In subsequent chapters, it is assumed that the development of statutory and voluntary services must proceed in close collaboration.

7 ORGANISING MENTAL HEALTH SERVICES

District responsibility

Community mental health services are necessary in order to provide help that is not ordinarily available in the locality or that is available but cannot be utilised because of mental disorder. The three principles underlying these provisions are district responsibility, comprehensive coverage and continuity of care.

The extent to which a 'community' cares for its own disabled members varies widely. Inner city areas are notoriously deficient in this respect; the residents of more affluent suburbs may be preoccupied with material standards that demand a conventional normality; even supposedly socially integrated rural villages may fall short of romantic expectation. Neighbours do not always help or even sympathise with the problems of the family containing a mentally ill member next door. Objections may be raised to plans for opening a local hostel or day centre, even when the users are completely harmless and well-ordered, on the grounds that the amenities and financial values of the neighbourhood will suffer. Severe mental illness is frightening and alienating, not only to those who suffer it, but to those who do not. The temptation to avoid thinking about it, let alone trying to understand and help, is strong. Formal systems of service delivery developed 'because the informal networks of mutual aid in local communities were manifestly incapable of meeting the kinds of personal need which arise in complex industrial societies'.[1]

This general tendency is compounded by the fact that severe mental illnesses often lead to difficulties in making and sustaining social relationships. Moreover, affected people may not be able to use ordinary amenities—shops, parks, pubs, libraries and so on—without special help.

Authorities with a statutory duty to provide mental health services therefore have a double task. First, they are responsible for mobilising local support, for health education, for liaison with neighbourhood and voluntary organisations, and with other statutory services (police, employment, housing, social security and so on), for adapting local facilities so that disabled people can use them, and for providing amenities that both disabled and other people can share. Secondly, they are responsible for identifying and meeting need through the provision of special services, with special relevance to mental health.

These duties demand a thorough knowledge of the local district and its characteristics. The anonymity of inner urban areas attracts people with few social roots and increases the alienation of disabled people who do belong locally. Rural areas have completely different problems, with transport and communications and outward migration of ambitious residents. Nevertheless, the underlying principles are universally applicable, though they must be adapted in practice according to the social context of each unique district.

Only through the application of these principles can any meaning be given to the concept of 'community care', which is otherwise a mere slogan.

Above all, we believe that the development of statutory responsibility for identifying and meeting needs within geographically defined districts is the correct way to proceed. *This is the first principle.* The rest of the chapter is devoted to an examination of ways in which this development can be improved and accelerated.

The responsibility divided

The two authorities with statutory responsibility for providing mental health care are District Health Authorities of the National Health Service and Social Service Departments of local government. District Health Authorities are funded out of taxes and there is a clear line of management from the Secretary of State, through Regional Health Authorities, to each district committee (the members of which are appointed to represent various interests) served by a community physician, district administrator and district treasurer. Local doctors, nurses and other staff are represented on a network of specialist committees. Central priorities and directives can therefore affect local services. By the same token, remote planners may lay down guidelines that ignore the tremendous variation in characteristics and in need between districts. However, the capacity of the Department of Health and Social Security to change the details of local expenditure is strictly limited. Several Secretaries of State, over the years, have tried to increase the proportion spent on mental health services, without much success.

The local authority committee concerned with social services is composed of elected members and is responsible to the local electorate. In this sense, community responsibility should be ensured. The Director of the Social Services Department heads a hierarchy of social workers and other staff. The department is financed partly from the rates plus a proportion, decided by the local authority, of the money allocated from central government. The personal social services cover accommodation, help in daily living and interpersonal relations, transport, recreation, training and sheltered employment. The main beneficiaries are the elderly and children. The mentally ill come bottom of the list, both in terms of money spent and in terms of the attitudes of staff. A study of the attitudes of field social workers showed that the mentally ill, mentally retarded and elderly severely mentally infirm were given lowest priority.

The two systems are doubly interdependent. For example, if the local authority does not provide for an elderly person who cannot stay at home, the pressure for providing care shifts to the District Health Authority, and elderly people accumulate in hospital because there is no alternative.

Moreover, there is commonly a split within the local authority itself. The Social Services Department is responsible for general planning and provision of services but the statutory duty to provide for homeless people falls on the Housing Department. This duty has often been interpreted to mean providing any sort of 'roof', and the temptation to allocate accommodation in otherwise 'hard to let' housing, particularly in inner city areas, has led to concentrations of people with various kinds of social problems, including mental illness, in certain estates. Close co-operation between the Housing and Social Services Departments can ensure good selection and supervision as well as the simple provision of premises and there are a few examples, such as in the London borough of Redbridge, demonstrating what can be done for the mentally ill in this way.[22] The benefits to the Housing Department through a lessening of problems such as socially unacceptable behaviour and rent arrears, and to the Health Authority by decreasing the pressure on beds, makes for cost-effectiveness. Unfortunately, co-operative efforts of this kind are still rare.

A fundamental principle is that, throughout the whole range of problems that occur in association with mental disorders, the boundary between what is 'medical' and what is 'social' is extremely difficult to draw. Although there are two distinct systems for providing care the range of problems is continuous.

District Health Authorities and Social Service Departments should have co-terminous boundaries, usually counties or urban boroughs. In practice, many do not, which leads to endless administrative problems. Moreover, some large mental hospitals may cater for several District Health Authorities and Social Service Departments. Though 'sectorisation' of the hospitals can simplify some problems, it can give rise to others, particularly when trying to administer the hospital as a whole. However, as we shall explain in Chapter 9, the basic geographical unit should be the Health District if this is the administrative unit through which funds would be channelled in order to develop the community services further.

The team concept has been developed in order to help co-ordinate health and social work staff assessments and the allocation of services. Social workers thus become involved in decisions concerning in-patients, day-patients and out-patients and, conversely, consultant psychiatrists or community psychiatric nurses may visit day centres and hostels run by the local authority. These efforts at co-ordination are fragmentary at best and there are numerous examples of people whose needs are not met by either system.

A general practitioner called a psychiatrist for consultation because a patient, recently discharged from hospital, was overactive and odd in behaviour at home. The specialist said the patient should be attending a day centre (though he refused to go) and that social services should be contacted. The family doctor arranged for a social worker to call but was told that it was a matter for the hospital services. Meanwhile, the relatives had to cope as best they could.

Voluntary organisations do their best to fill the gaps and often undertake some of the functions of both statutory services. They are not responsible, however, in the sense that the two statutory services are for the needs of the district. Both statutory systems, but particularly the SSDs, are pressed for money and have had to make cuts. This means that priorities have had to become even sharper than before and that the low position occupied by the mental health services has further deteriorated. We believe that the voluntary services can play a far more active role, as suggested in Chapter 6, but that it is essential to provide, as a statutory requirement, a minimal pattern into which they can fit.

Comprehensive coverage

Each ill or disabled person has a unique pattern of needs. *The second principle* of good community care is that services must be flexible enough to be able to cater for this variety. In the old days, most functions were carried out on one hospital site. If the hospital was remote from the area it served it was impossible to provide day care without the patient having to live on a ward. Conversely, it might be difficult to provide night-time care and allow the resident to work outside hospital. Some hospitals did manage to overcome these limitations but only for relatively few patients. All the functions carried out by those hospitals still have to be undertaken, as well as several new ones. Only a brief outline can be given here.

We suggested, earlier in this chapter, that there are 'positive' community functions, including fostering public awareness, particularly among opinion leaders, mobilising community support, co-ordinating voluntary efforts, seeking promising local initiatives, using publicly available amenities such as evening classes, sharing community responsibility. Local Associations of Mental Health, branches of the National Schizophrenia Fellowship, and voluntary organisations supplying services in the district are insufficiently brought into this important activity. The better the community relations, the simpler it is to identify need.

A smoothly functioning emergency service is one of the key elements in provision partly because of the public exposure in crises involving the mentally ill. A crisis intervention team including psychiatrist, nurse and social worker, based on the local hospital, which has developed close relationships with local general practitioners, the police and other relevant community agencies, can save much suffering and embarrassment to patient and family, ensure early treatment and minimise the need for hospital care. Domiciliary visiting, which allows a realistic assessment of the problems within the social setting, has long been a feature of both health and social services and provides a basis for crisis intervention.

Treatment services—in hospital wards, day hospital, out-patient clinics and through community psychiatric nurses—should be based in the psychiatric units of district general hospitals. This has been part of the government's plans since 1961 but only one third of all patients are admitted to such units. Day hospitals should be able to treat certain emergencies if home or residential care is otherwise adequate, thus preventing hospital admission, but this practice is not universal. Similarly, the possibility of admission to a hostel or 'retreat' is rarely available, although not everyone who has to leave home for a while because of acute mental distress needs to be in hospital.

A broad range of other day and residential units is also required, providing a network of combinations of care that will cater for most patterns of need. A substantial proportion of people living in hostels, group homes, subsidised housing or boarding-out schemes also need sheltered day-time occupation. This may take the form of day centres with mainly social and recreational functions, industrial therapy units or sheltered workshops. Above all, facilities must offer opportunities for friendships and mutual support.

We discussed in Chapter 4 the necessity for imagination in providing leisure-time activities for those who are unable, by reason of their disabilities, to organise their own. Restaurant and social clubs, such as those set up by the Psychiatric Rehabilitation Association, with its evening groups and weekend activities, provide a model. Other facilities are needed for people who require both night-time and day-time shelter and who cannot travel from one to another on public transport. There are positive aspects to the concept of 'asylum' that remain when the negative connotations associated with the custodial era have been eliminated.

The needs for counselling and advice have also been described in Chapter 4. They cover information on numerous aspects of mental disorder, including causes, treatment and long-term management, living with disability, welfare benefits, liaison and work opportunities, and the allocation of services. This is one of the areas most complained about in 'consumer' surveys and will receive more attention in Chapter 8, where we deal with training. The other basic problem arises from a lack of co-ordination and integration of the caring services which is considered in the next section.

This comprehensive coverage is nowhere available in the United Kingdom. While deploring the lack of alternatives we consider that no hospital should be closed until the alternatives are available and shown to be working well.

Minimal service requirements

In order to achieve decent standards of community care, it is necessary to lay down minimal levels of provision to be aimed for in every Health District in the country. These must be couched in broad terms since, as we have argued earlier, several different patterns of service could be effective. However, the minimal guidelines suggested in the Government White Paper of 1975, which have still not been implemented, are sufficiently broad to cover the essentials.[7] We do not believe that they are adequate, but if they could be achieved, there would at least be a basis for the development of a comprehensive service. (We are not here concerned with the elderly mentally infirm or mentally retarded.)

The guidelines (per 100,000 of the population) are as follows:

Beds in district general hospitals	50
Day hospital places	25
Hostel-wards for 'new' long-stay	17
Short-term and rehabilitation hostels . . .	4—6
Long-stay accommodation in staffed and unstaffed homes and supervised lodgings .	15—24
Day centre places	60

Staffing levels, too, vary widely from one district to another. The Department suggested minimum levels for nurses and social workers in 1972 but many districts have not yet achieved even these. We suggest that the duty of health and social service authorities to provide adequate numbers of places and of staff, and adequate quality of care, should be specified by statute and that a designated Minister should be given responsibility for ensuring that a good standard is met (see Chapter 9). So far, Section 12 of the 1968 Health and Public Services Act, which requires local authorities to provide for the care and after-care of the mentally ill, has not been enforced.

In addition to these basic needs, it is clear that innovative changes are required as suggested in Chapters 4 and 5:

(i)   day centres intermediate in level between 'occupational therapy' and 'sheltered workshops';

(ii)   at least some high-level sheltered factories;

(iii)   rehabilitation units of various kinds, where disturbed or disabled people can be prepared for independent living in group homes and bedsitters;

(iv)   hostels that are available for refuge rather than for treatment.

Modification to the principle of district responsibility

So far, we have assumed that all the services needed should be provided within the district where ill or disabled people live. Several qualifications must be made to this rule.

It is essential to provide a degree of choice. There may be only one unit of a particular kind within a district and there will usually be no more than three consultant psychiatrists (using the same wards). It is legitimate for an individual or for a relative to request a second opinion, or a service outside the district, if there is reason to be dissatisfied with what is provided locally, or if nothing is provided at all. Voluntary organisations can help but cannot be expected to take full responsibility. The statutory services should be flexible enough to be able to cope with such situations without cavil.

Primary medical services (see Chapter 3) are not completely district-based and general practitioners are free to refer patients to any service they think appropriate. This, together with the ability to seek a second opinion, is a valuable function which must be preserved.

Occasionally, it may occur that an afflicted individual puts down roots in a day or residential unit or a sheltered community, and has no wish to move, even though members of the family may do so. Such a person should continue to be a resident of the district. The most familiar example, of course, is the individual who has grown old in a mental hospital and has no wish to move elsewhere simply because relatives have done so. There are now equivalents in the alternative community services.

An analogous problem is provided by people who 'sleep rough', or settle down in long-stay annexes attached to reception centres or in Salvation Army hostels. They have no roots in any local community and the local authority does not feel responsible for them.* In some inner city areas there are many people like this and it is unfair to charge the local services for providing decent accommodation and occupational facilities for them. Nevertheless, it is inhuman to expect them to move on. Special funding is required to enable the district to include them in its service provision (see Chapter 9).

Some problems are too uncommon to justify the provision of a special service in every district. This would be true, for example, of the sheltered communities that we would like to see set up on an experimental basis, and which would include activities such as horticulture, horse-riding and sports. Two or three districts acting together, however, should be able to provide suitable facilities. The essence of the matter is that there must be a place of last resort, when every other refuge fails.

These exceptions can be catered for without the principles of district responsibility being abrogated.

Administration and organisation

One of our themes in this Report has been that different patterns of service can equally well, or equally badly, serve the aims of community responsibility and that the presence of services, and professional people to staff them, does not mean that the needs of disabled people and their families are being met. Motivation and training of staff (see Chapter 8), and good organisation are essential. The latter implies effective management of each component of the services and integration into a system with no serious gaps, no serious blocks to transfer between units (which would provide a range of choices, not institutional dead ends) and no falling off of commitment when disabled people continue to need care over many years.

Organisational problems arise at many levels. We shall consider four—those of the individual (and family), the staff team, the service unit and the district. Regional and national levels will be considered in Chapter 9.

The individual and the family

At the individual level there are two apparently different problems—coping with a crisis and coping with the longer-term problems that accompany mental disability. The two are often related, however, because crises can often be predicted, though not precisely, from a knowledge of the clinical history and, even when they arise out of the blue, previous events are usually highly relevant. The main problems with clinical emergencies arise when they occur 'out of hours' and the

* The 'single homeless' have a far lower priority than homeless families.

staff who know about the individual's problems are off duty. The organisation of 'on call' services leaves much to be desired, as general practitioners know very well.

We commend the suggestion put forward by the multidisciplinary Working Party on Psychiatric Rehabilitation convened by the Royal College of Psychiatrists[21] that there should be a register of people at risk in each district, for each of whom a key worker or care-coordinator should be identified. This worker would be able to mobilise services and resources without hierarchical decision-making interrupting the programme. This would only be possible if all the trained caring staff available to District Health Authorities, Social Services Departments and local voluntary organisations took part in the scheme. An element of common training would be essential (see Chapter 8) and the levels of organisation to be considered below would have to be functioning properly. For example, a staff member in one system (say a community nurse) would have to be familiar with the whole range of services available, including those provided by other systems (Social Services Departments, etc.) and to be able to draw upon them or to make a referral to the appropriate worker. At present, administrative and professional barriers often prevent this apparently elementary arrangement from being implemented.

The advantage of such an arrangement is that people on the register would always be able to call on someone who was familiar with the relevant circumstances. Since care coordinators could not be available all the time it would be necessary to rely on stand-ins as well but these should be drawn, as far as possible, from the same staff team. Even in an emergency during unsocial hours, it should be possible to find a knowledgeable—and discreet—member of staff.

The staff team

Because of the disparate needs of mentally ill or disabled people, a range of different professions has developed, each claiming an expertise in some aspect of care. We are not convinced that quite so many specialisms are justified but, for the moment, it is necessary to discuss the organisational aspects of bringing their various skills to bear on the problems of individual people in need. The chief specialist professions concerned are psychiatry, nursing (hospital and community), social work (of various kinds), clinical psychology, and occupational therapy or training.

A disadvantage of the team concept is that it could lead to endless discussion between protagonists of different (perhaps partial) points of view, so that no decision was reached or, if there were a consensus, it would be nobody's responsibility to carry it into action. Such havering is encouraged if there is no team leader. In virtually every service setting it is clear where the leadership, and therefore the responsibility, should lie.

If this problem can be solved, the advantages of the team concept are overwhelming. The multifarious nature of need has been sufficiently emphasised already. It can only be met by the prescription of a variety of forms of help. Expertise is most valuable when it is harnessed to the solution of specific problems. If one member of the team is appointed key worker (with the consent of the individual and family concerned), all the various kinds of expertise available can be welded into an overall plan, the execution of which is delegated to one member of staff. Team reviews of each individual should be regular but need not be frequent. Most of the time staff members will be acting on their initiative within the framework of the overall plan.

Conversely, all members of staff should be part of, or attached to, a team. This will help overcome the isolation felt by the staff of small, geographically fragmented, and possibly socially isolated, units and will contribute to the development of a common approach to care. There is much to be said for finding ways of bringing the staff of local voluntary organisations that provide overlapping services into such a system.

Team work creates problems of its own. However, many of the problems that surface in multidisciplinary groups can be circumvented when regular meetings are maintained at which members can consider their cases with colleagues. Personal conflicts may be expressed in various ways and sharing cases brings out the common human reactions to adverse social circumstances, whether in the family or in a wider social setting.

Service units and their management

Each unit (ward, hostel, day centre, out-patient clinic, etc.) will have one or more staff teams for the care of attenders. Most units are managed through a hierarchical system. District Health Authorities and Social Services Departments have their own administrative and professional bureaucracies which have developed over a long period of time but are not necessarily suited to the requirements of a community care system. The major problems are lack of staff continuity and staff responsibility.

Lack of continuity is partly due to the training requirements of nurses and social workers, who need to gain experience in a variety of settings. It is also due to staff shortages, so that people have to be moved at short notice to cover gaps. Sometimes, however, it appears to be almost built into the system because it is easy for management to forget the importance of staff–client relationships when making staff dispositions.

The management of units is often more cumbersome than it need be and offers less to the initiative and responsibility of the unit staff than seems desirable. The problems of hierarchical direction are most obvious in a small unit. A useful comparison can be made with a school, where the head teacher has a clear responsibility for spending the budget allocated, for recruiting staff and for everyday running of affairs. There are restrictions of many kinds but, within these, much scope for initiative. To become Head is sufficient ambition for most teachers, who would not regard a subsequent move into a purely administrative position as promotion. This is less true in nursing or in social work.

A further requirement would be that clear operating policies were laid down for units, in respect of selection procedures, treatment and care objectives and quality of environment provided. At the moment, these policies often develop by trial and error. Admission and discharge policies may be adopted that are very difficult to change and movement between units may be very difficult to achieve.

Organising such a complex array of statutory and non-statutory elements into an integrated mental health service is a problem that has defeated all efforts so far. A promising idea is 'core and cluster' organisation, in which one unit (day or residential), with a wide range of treatment, rehabilitation and sheltered work functions, acts as the centre to which are attached smaller peripheral day and residential units. This overcomes the problem of isolation of staff in geographically separated houses, which it is just as important to avoid as the isolation of clients. Training, team discussions, continuity of care and access of personal counsellors to a wide range of other staff and services is facilitated.

To make service co-ordination effective a district co-ordinator is needed, supported by a multi-professional group whose members are influential within the services they represent. The committee should be accessible to all field workers and to clients and relatives. It should be responsible for compiling a register of those in long-term need in the district. The grass roots experience of members as to how units and personal services were functioning would lead to specific recommendations for development within the district. The coordinator could be any professional, but it is essential that he or she should be able to provide long-term continuity, should be able to take substantial responsibility, provide leadership and be able to influence all the component parts of the services.

The co-ordinator could be the consultant psychiatrist with a special responsibility for community services or a senior SSD worker, or a nurse with substantial experience in the field. Part of the co-ordinator's function would be to institute a simple basic assessment routine in all units. Field workers would be responsible for reporting cases in which services were not appropriate to needs but where they were unable to take the action necessary to resolve the mismatch. Intervention or assistance from the co-ordinator would then be required, either at the regular review or in an emergency.

These measures would, of course, do no more than patch up a system where responsibility for mental health care is still fundamentally divided and sub-divided. Members of the Enquiry are convinced that moves must be made towards achieving a more unified service. Although such an evolution is likely to take a long time, some small steps have already been taken in the right direction and the time seems right for further progress to be made.

At present there is a statutory obligation on health and local authorities to collaborate through Joint Consultative Committees which can set up Joint Care Planning Teams to work in specified areas such as mental health. Joint funding arrangements have been introduced whereby National Health Service money can be used for mutually agreed projects, usually quite small, in the statutory or voluntary services. Capital costs, and running costs tapering off from three to seven years, with rare extensions to thirteen years, are now covered but eventually the revenue costs will come home to roost and resources may not then be available. Moreover, although the Joint Care Planning Teams can make suggestions, the social service input is often at too junior a level and recommendations may carry little weight even if they get to the Social Services Committee.

We think that our proposed system based on personal care co-ordinators, staff teams, and better managed units represented within a multi-disciplinary committee led by a district co-ordinator, would be more in touch with local needs, more aware of gaps in services and better able to make suggestions for improvement than the present Joint Care Planning Teams. No movement towards providing an integrated service would be likely to be successful, however, unless there were an identifiable mental health budget, the spending of which could be directly influenced by the committee. If this could eventually be achieved, we should be moving in the direction of a *de facto* mental health service, although the main structure of the two statutory services would be unaltered. We consider how to identify a mental health budget in Chapter 9.

We suggest that each District needs a Joint Mental Health Development Committee, with senior representatives from the main services involved, both Health and Local Authority, and that there should also be representation of local voluntary services. The mechanism need not be specified here, although if there is a local body coordinating the efforts of the voluntary services, it might be the appropriate group to make the election. It would be particularly important that the Social Services Department representative should be senior enough to carry weight with the Social Services Committee.

We further suggest that this committee should be given certain financial duties, which are specified in Chapter 9, together with suggestions about the line of authority to a specified Minister in DHSS. Without some link to finance, we doubt whether even the organisation we have outlined would be able to accelerate progress towards good community care.

Monitoring standards

The organisational structure suggested here would need to be monitored. Once minimal criteria were laid down it would be the task of the Joint Mental Health Development Committee to see that they were met, but this would, of course, only provide a basic level on which to develop further. The quality of care is as important as the quantity. We have argued that most day and residential units should adopt operating policies designed to ensure that each unit fits into an overall pattern of high quality care while, at the same time, allowing for the exercise of individual initiative and responsibility. This is the case with schools, for example, which are monitored through management committees, an inspectorate and parent–teacher associations. We suggest that similar arrangements are needed in the mental health service.

The system by which Her Majesty's Inspectors have raised the general level of education in this country is widely known and appreciated. Although there are certain statutory powers, the influence of the inspectors has been largely moral. Critical reports are taken seriously. The nucleus of such an inspectorate is present in the Health Advisory Service and the Social Work Service Officers for Regions, although their functions should be considerably strengthened so that they can report on standards and on value-for-money throughout the mental health services. The Government has suggested that the inspectorial functions of the Social Work Service should be strengthened and we welcome this initiative. However, we should like to see a movement towards a joint (or coordinated) Health and Social Services Inspectorate that would monitor the quantitative and qualitative levels of care in each District, compared with the national standard, and report to the Mental Health Development Committee and to the DHSS. In Chapter 9, we consider the sanctions that might be imposed if standards were found wanting.

Management committees have not proved unduly intrusive in the educational system and we think they would play an important role, by bringing a variety of experienced opinion to bear, in the health and social services also. Voluntary organisations representing patients and their relatives, and Community Health Councils, should also be encouraged to take a constructive interest in the standards reached by local services.

Finally, 'health and social services research', which is a neglected field in this country, can provide an independent evaluation of the strengths and weaknesses of local services and thus prove invaluable for local planning. A budget for such research (which should not, of course, be administered by the authorities under investigation) is as important for the development of the mental health services as it is for any other large enterprise.

Summary

The aims of a community mental health service are to prevent or ameliorate the effects of disease, disability, disadvantage and distress, in order to enable patients or clients who contact the service to achieve their own personal goals as far as that is possible. 'Community care' is thus defined in positive terms rather than as a mere shift away from large hospitals.

A good service should be based on the principles of district responsibility, comprehensive provision and continuity of care. This means that minimal standards of provision must be laid down—covering medical treatment and care, residential and day units. Adequate numbers of trained and experienced staff should be available.

In order to create an integrated service it is necessary to ensure that people who are at risk of serious disorder or long-term disability, and their relatives, should be able to call on a personal care coordinator. Multidisciplinary teams of staff should be able to cover all the needs likely to be present and help overcome the fragmentation inherent in the separate development of health, social and voluntary services and the barriers between different professions. Day and residential units require a management system that allows staff to exercise more responsibility and more initiative. We suggest how this might be done.

It is essential that there is plenty of opportunity for choice between services, and that the principle of district responsibility should not be interpreted so narrowly that movement across boundaries is discouraged, second opinions are rarely sought, people with no 'parish of origin' are not provided for and units that serve two or more districts are not created.

We suggest a new type of management system for community mental health services—a Joint Mental Health Development Committee on which all the local interests are represented by senior members, able to influence policy within their own authorities but also closely in touch with problems emerging at individual, team and unit level. The Committee would not only attempt to meet the minimum standards laid down but do so in the light of the principles laid out in this chapter. The financial implications are considered in Chapter 9.

Monitoring the success of local services in meeting standards and providing a good quality of care should be undertaken by a new Inspectorate with duties equivalent to those of Her Majesty's Inspectors of Schools. Methods of local monitoring are also outlined.

8 PROFESSIONAL EXPERIENCE AND TRAINING

General principles

Throughout this Report, we have emphasised the fact that the mere provision of service units (wards, out-patient clinics, day centres, a domiciliary service, etc.) does not in itself ensure an adequate service; it is simply the essential basis for one. Two other essentials are required: (a) organisation according to the principles of responsible, comprehensive and integrated community care (Chapter 7); (b) staff who understand the nature of the multifarious problems experienced by and posed by people with severe mental illness and disability (Chapter 2), are familiar with the ways in which these problems can more effectively be alleviated (Chapters 4 and 6) and able to plan and allocate the appropriate services.

The three elements of service provision, proper organisation and staff training are closely interdependent, a fact that does not make for clear exposition. In this chapter, we shall concentrate on the third essential—staff with the right knowledge and skills, including the ability to make use of the whole available range of community services. We do not propose to deal in detail with questions of curricula, since useful expositions are already available from professional bodies and multidisciplinary groups. There are, however, several general issues to which we think insufficient attention has been given. The first includes the motivation and attitudes of staff; the second concerns the balance between education and apprenticeship; the third is the question of specialisation versus 'generic' training. These three issues are inseparable.

The question of motivation is bound up with that of selection. All professions are aware of the problem. Some people seem to make 'natural' doctors, nurses or social workers; outstanding academic prowess is not at all essential though it is certainly not inimical. Others may have good paper qualifications but find it difficult to put knowledge into practice when faced with clients or patients. Most people come somewhere in between. It has at times been argued that selecting the right people is more important than the nature of the training they receive in nursing or in social work: apprenticeship in a good practice is all that is necessary. Without going so far, we consider that selection is vital at every stage of training and that academic qualifications are insufficient in themselves to identify suitable professional

72

people. We place great value, therefore, on the assessment of personal qualities during the apprenticeship. This is particularly important in professions, such as psychiatric nursing and social work, where it is difficult to find niches for those high in academic but low in psycho-social skills.

Social skills are of little value if thought of as 'techniques' or pre-scribed procedures for common situations. The ability to give help with the emotional aspects of personal problems—as distinct from pro-viding relevant information—depends on the maturity of the coun-sellor. It is, therefore, essential to provide an opportunity to gain experience of such help from experienced supervisors. The academic component in training provides knowledge about specific social and psychological problems, but this knowledge needs to be used by some-one with confidence in his or her own ability to cope with adversity and to respond to human problems in such a way as to assure clients that their own particular problems are fully understood and need not be overwhelming.

A further reason for emphasising the apprenticeship part of train-ing is that one of the essential elements in good community care is the allocation and utilisation of services. This may best be learned by experience in several well-functioning multidisciplinary teams. It can-not be taught in a classroom, although the principles can be made explicit. The DHSS has recognised a few 'centres of excellence' where experience of psychiatric rehabilitation can be gained. (The term 'rehabilitation' has a broad connotation here—it does *not* mean ex-perience in an isolated 'rehabilitation ward'.) Accreditation schemes of various kinds exist for all the caring professions but none is based in the way we advocate, i.e. on good overall community care, with well-run units functioning as part of a responsible, comprehensive and integrated district service. It is true that few such services exist but to recognise the best of them is already to set standards, to raise them further in the best districts and to encourage trainees to strive to emulate them elsewhere.

The problem of specialised versus generic training is more con-veniently considered in the context of an even wider issue—that of the separate development of the professions.

Common problems but separate professions

As we pointed out in Chapter 1, there was once a kind of unified mental health service, one with many disadvantages and limitations but nevertheless operating under a single administrative umbrella. The mental hospitals were administered by local authorities, and medi-cal, nursing, social work and occupational functions were carried out on one site. External social work was the responsibility of Duly Authorised Officers (later Mental Welfare Officers) who were usually based in the local authority medical department.

Diversification has taken the form of separate professional and administrative development. In particular, various groups have sought association with a learned profession; adopting its standards, its broader vision (since severe mental illness forms a very small part of the interest of most professions), its audit of practice, its status and the morale-enhancing company of other members. These advantages are indeed to be prized but it is important to recognise, and try to circumvent, the disadvantages that accompany them.

There is a tendency, for example, for each profession to emphasise a type of assessment and care which only its members are said to be qualified to give. Thus 'casework' and 'community work' seem to become the prerogative of social workers. Cognitive and attitude testing, behaviour therapy and programming become regarded as the sole province of clinical psychologists. Occupational therapists are seen as specialists only in vocational and recreational activities. Nurses, who used to undertake all these other tasks to some extent, appear to be left with the exercise of basic nursing care or the management of severely disturbed behaviour, for which roles they have few rivals. Doctors may seem to be relegated to diagnosis and physical treatment. This is a caricature of what actually occurs and a travesty of what each profession claims for itself but it illustrates a real danger.

Isolated professional training relegates mental illness to a low place in a 'generic' plan of training and, at the same time, provides a model for approaching it so restricted in scope that long post-graduate experience is needed to learn how and when the special techniques can most effectively be used in a general plan of treatment. Unless this experience is acquired in the right kind of apprenticeship, there is a serious risk that each type of professional will formulate the problems of the mentally ill merely in terms of his or her own particular techniques, undervalue the skills of other professionals, and avoid altogether the range of 'mundane' needs to which patients and relatives give high priority—finding a job, getting better housing, acquiring vocational or domestic skills, becoming better informed about the service options available, and knowing what to do in various emergencies. The best way to tackle problems like destitution (more than a third of the 'single homeless' are or have been severely mentally ill), or to provide a decent standard of sheltered work in every district, will not be learned during an academic course in psychology or social work.

One of the problems commonly raised by relatives illustrates the fact that we are not here discussing a theoretical risk but one which all too often becomes reality.

A mother says:

'My son comes home from the day centre, goes straight up to his room, locks the door, pulls the curtains and lies on his bed in the dark, smoking and talking to himself. What should I do?'

Another mother says:

'My daughter will not use her bedroom because she says that the neighbours are pumping gas into the room. What should I do?'

In each case a relative has several options. Staff with different kinds of training will have different ways of formulating the problems, and their own favoured techniques of assessment and counselling or psychotherapy. None, however, will necessarily give practical advice to the relatives. Both mothers, in fact, said that no useful reply was received from any of the professional people asked. The commonest answer was 'What *did* you do?'. When the mothers themselves explained the alternatives they had considered and described the failure of their own trial-and-error solutions, no further constructive advice was obtained.[18]

Members of the Enquiry are not impressed with the idea of creating a new type of worker—a mental health professional—as has been tried in some areas in the United States. This is to combine the disadvantages of old and new without obtaining the benefits of either. In any case, professional loyalties are too strong. The solution we advocate is to strengthen the specialist (mental health) aspect of academic training for all relevant professions, with some courses taken in common, and to emphasise the importance of apprentice training in multidisciplinary and other specialist teams in accredited centres, chosen because the overall context of community care is, or promises to be, excellent.

If the recommendations for the organisation of district services made in chapter 7 were accepted, it would become much easier to base part of the specialist training of each profession on the work of the various multiprofessional teams and to require involvement as an apprentice in several specialist placements before granting a specialist qualification. Common elements in the various academic courses would then be more conveniently brought together so that at least some of the training would be shared.

The central core of training

The common elements have already been mentioned in previous chapters and need only be summarised here by way of reminder. The basis of the training must be to acquire an understanding of the nature of the problems causing or commonly accompanying severe mental illness, including the way these are experienced by the individual affected, by relatives and by society more generally. These problems are complex because of the interaction of factors due to disorder, disability, disadvantage and distress. The principles of help and care are based on this understanding. Each profession will naturally focus on its own specialist 'therapies' but the task of a common training will be to show how each kind of treatment or care or help can be fitted into an overall plan. The allocation, management and organisation of service units follows naturally when this basic understanding of problems and options has been acquired. Within the framework of the local services, teaching will emphasise the principles of district responsibility, comprehensive coverage and continuity of care, facilitated by discussion of local characteristics, such as the distribution of age, types of housing and occupation, birth and death rates, migration in and out of the district, patterns of psychiatric disorder, and so on. The personal care coordinator scheme advocated in Chapter 7 will only be possible if all the caring professionals in the district are trained and utilised.

It would take us too far from the field of enquiry with which we are principally concerned to go further into detail about the content and administration of this training. More detailed suggestions are made elsewhere. [4,15,21,24] The aim, however, is clear. It is to further the development of a true mental health service by overcoming the disadvantages inherent in the separation of professional functions and training.

In the following two sections we deal with social work and nursing by way of illustrating the general principles enunciated so far. In a recent compendium on psychiatric rehabilitation, contributions by nurses, social workers and occupational therapists illustrated the fundamental point we wish to emphasise—how much overlap there is, in practice, between the roles adopted by the various professions. Nevertheless, each contributor regarded his or her profession as the one that was chiefly concerned with rehabilitation. It is only if this overlap is seen to be a firm basis for integration of effort, rather than an area for indiscriminate take-over by one or other school of thought, that the principles of community care can truly be practised.

Social work

The Barclay Report[1] concluded that social workers do a great many helpful things that would otherwise be left undone, to the detriment of those in need. Very little was said in the report either about the particular problems of the severely mentally ill or about training social workers to cope with these problems. This is in line with the generally low priority given to the mentally ill and the current emphasis on a generic (non-specialist) approach.

Social workers with a psychiatric training (Psychiatric Social Workers) used to be the elite of the social work profession in the days when little other education was available. For many years they were 'the only group of social workers in Britain whose professional training was exclusively based in the universities, which gave them a degree of prestige and professional scarcity denied to their colleagues in other fields'.[13] Indeed many social workers in other fields took the Psychiatric Social Work course at the London School of Economics simply in order to acquire some training. Most Psychiatric Social Workers worked in hospital departments of social work.

Before the unification of all social work (except probation) in one local authority Social Services Department, there were specialist workers known as Mental Welfare Officers, usually employed in the health or welfare department. Some were Psychiatric Social Workers, others had been psychiatric nurses, but most were untrained. They did, however, acquire considerable experience, particularly in relation to the provisions of the Mental Health Act (1959) concerning compulsory admission to hospital. This limited but essential role was extended, in the case of some authorities, to more general after-care but, by and large, the MWOs had little contact with other social work activities.

In 1971, following the implementation of the Seebohm report, which recommended the creation of a single social work profession with a generic (non-specialised) training, Social Services Departments took over the functions of the former children's health and welfare departments. Many Mental Welfare Officers were recruited to social work qualifying courses but, on return, took up general duties rather than working with the mentally ill.

The 'generic' view of social work which was generally adopted at that time and is still influential now, assumes that the same basic principles of training and practice apply whatever the client group. The two-year courses leading to a Certificate of Qualification (one year for those with a relevant degree), inevitably give little attention to any particular speciality, and expertise in the psychiatric aspects (particularly with the severely mentally ill or disabled) has become much less common. We strongly recommend that there should be a one-year probation period following the acquisition of a Certificate of Qualification in Social Work before fully responsible practice is allowed.

In 1974, the Central Council for Education and Training in Social Work made some forthright recommendations concerning training and experience in various specific aspects of social work with physically and mentally disabled people (Handicapped People Need Better Trained Social Workers).[4] In particular, a specimen curriculum was appended which might form the basis of an advanced course dealing with psychiatric disability. The generic principle was still accepted but it was recognised that, as in medicine, many specialities were also needed.

Although there are now four 'specialist' psychiatric courses, the vast majority of social workers still obtain only the most exiguous training in meeting the needs of severely mentally ill people. It is often difficult for social workers to get the funds necessary to attend the specialist courses that do exist.

In 1975, the Central Council for Education and Training in Social Work introduced a new form of training; a modular course with continuous assessment which, if successfully completed, met the standards for the Certificate of Social Service. Three modules formed a *common unit* taken by everyone. In addition, there was a *standard unit* in which each student was invited to choose from some broad but discrete areas of study and a *specialised* option which could be specifically concerned with a subject such as mental illness or mental handicap. The idea was excellent but much of the original concept was not realised in the subsequent courses. It was never accepted as a general professional qualification and has, in consequence, been obtained chiefly by the staff of residential and day care units for various handicapped groups. Thus the staff of such units for the mentally ill and disabled can acquire an adequate basic training (better in respect of their speciality than that of generically trained staff) but this has no impact on field social work outside these units; nor is someone with a Certificate of Social Service allowed to undertake the field social work duties of someone with a Certificate of Qualification in Social Work. A further disadvantage of downgrading the Certificate of Social Service from the level originally envisaged is that a range of specialist modules, taught in centres of excellence, and available to all social workers who are interested in a particular specialist subject, has not been developed. Workers with the Certificate of Qualification in Social Work have little encouragement to become expert in an area of their choice in addition to their general training.

Another point needs to be kept in mind when assessing the value of these certificates. Residential work requires staff to work unsocial hours. There is less competition for such jobs and the more competent people can, if they wish, choose less demanding work. Thus they miss the particularly intense and physical experience of residential work and may not understand what it means to cope, for example, with incontinence. The role of staff with a residential qualification is much closer to that of relatives and they become proportionately more understanding. Greater status should, therefore, be given to posts in day and residential units and the experience they provide should be given the same value as experience in field social work.

It is possibly due to the lack of specialist training that so many Social Services Departments adopt a policy of not providing social work help unless it is asked for by an identified client, or unless a particular, usually statutory, priority exists. Many people with severe mental illness, as we have seen in Chapter 2, are slow, underactive, socially withdrawn and lacking in motivation. This does not mean that they can be ignored until a 'statutory' emergency arises. It is likely that a pertinent clause in the Mental Health (Amendment) Act 1982, will provide a new statutory priority, with its designation of approved mental health social workers. However, it will be essential for the Central Council for Education and Training in Social Work to be given funds for setting up more specialist courses and providing more bursaries if local authorities are expected to fulfil the conditions of the Act.

It is hardly surprising that the relatives of the severely mentally ill tend to place the help given by social workers at the bottom of their list of effective care received. All too often, the minimal principle laid down by the Director of one Social Services Department—that the counsellor should know at least as much about the disability as the person counselled and the close relatives—is far from being met.

Members of the Enquiry find it astonishing that the principle of specialist courses for social workers is still not widely accepted. We suggest that the recommendations of the Central Council for Education and Training in Social Work Paper No. 5 are still valid and need urgently to be put into practice. Social Services Departments must not be allowed to by-pass the spirit of the 1982 Mental Health Amendment Act by designating existing staff as 'approved Social Workers' without seconding them to the approved specialist training. In addition, if our recommendation that some day centres or residential units should form the 'core' of a 'cluster' of other services is accepted, it means that the staff of such core units need the same kind of basic training and experience (in addition to their specialist skills) as field social workers. This means that their training should be supplemented in order to bring their qualifications up to the general level.

Finally, we make the same point about social workers in charge of care units as about nurses in similar positions. This is a highly responsible job. It should be the high point of ambition for most people, not a stage on a journey to an administrative post. Not only do they need the kind of training we have specified but they must be aware of and act upon the principles of community responsibility, comprehensive coverage and integration discussed in Chapter 7.

Nursing

Nurses constitute the major staff resource for severely ill or chronically disabled people. The central role they play in the care of the acutely ill, throughout all phases of rehabilitation and in community care, has been recognised by a series of improvements in status, conditions of work and training, though there is yet some way to go. Their activities include basic nursing care (e.g. of the severely infirm), coping with severely disturbed behaviour and severe mental disability, providing a 'therapeutic' environment in ward, hostel or day hospital, behavioural therapy (a recently introduced specialism), the management of medication, social and vocational rehabilitation, counselling patients and relatives, and domiciliary visiting (including supervision of clients at group homes, hostels and day centres). They are prepared to work 'unsocial' hours. They work in a wide variety of settings—residential units, day units, out-patient clinics and in the community. They interact with all the other helping professions. Wherever the other professions are in short supply, they are left to fill the gaps.

Finally, and perhaps least appreciated even by nurses themselves, they 'stand in' for relatives when caring for the mentally afflicted. There is no job that nurses do that some relatives do not have to do at some time. Nurses are, of course, professionals, and can remain emotionally neutral in a way that some relatives understandably find difficult to achieve; they work shifts rather than being 'on duty' 24 hours a day, seven days a week; and they see a wide variety of patients rather than having to concentrate on one. These differences do not detract from their potential ability to see the problems as relatives do or from their potential capacity to act as experienced and practically informed counsellors.

We have already suggested, in Chapter 7, that the practice of promoting senior nurses to administrative positions can be carried too far. The most effective organisation of community care requires many of the people in senior management positions to remain involved in some 'clinical' (using the word in its broadest sense) duties. By providing experience of district responsibility at senior level, this would promote the right approach to apprenticeship, training and practice throughout all levels of the nursing service.

The structure of nurse training is already well-suited to the inclusion of the contents we advocate.[24] The syllabus for the Certificate of Mental Nursing is broad enough to accommodate a substantial element covering the community aspects of nursing, which includes not only domiciliary work but care in *all* settings that serve the district. There are also advanced modules, such as course 810 of the Joint Board of Clinical Nursing Studies. Degree and Diploma courses should necessarily provide instruction in community nursing in the broad sense. The model curriculum already referred to as an appropriate basis for specialist social work training[4] would need little modification for nurses and much of it could be taken in common, given professional and administrative will. Detailed suggestions regarding content are given in chapters 3, 7 and 10 of a recent book and chapter 14 contains examples of district services that, between them, cover most of the needs of the community.[29]

The apprenticeship aspect is more difficult to provide. The Department of Health and Social Security has designated a few 'centres of excellence' suitable for advanced training in psychiatric rehabilitation. It will take time and local leadership before it is practicable to expect most nurses to have had experience in several integrated, multiprofessional teams concerned with various aspects of community care with an overall framework of district responsibility. Nevertheless, the aim is clear.

Other professional staff

We have given most attention to the training requirements of social workers and nurses because they provide the major resource available to people with severe mental illness or chronic disability. Each of the other professional groups could be considered in the same detail but, since the same principles apply, we shall summarise our views in a few paragraphs.

For example, we endorse the view of a multidisciplinary group sponsored by the Royal College of Psychiatrists[21] that psychiatric rehabilitation and community care is part of general clinical psychiatry and does not require the creation of a new sub-specialty. However, certain essential tasks should be the special responsibility of one of the existing consultant psychiatrists in each Health District. These are planning, coordination, management and training. This would have important implications for training registrars and senior registrars in the social and community aspects of their clinical work. It is greatly to be deplored that some, at any rate, of the posts created in response to this recommendation, have been regarded as serving only the needs of long-stay in-patients, perhaps with the aid of a 'rehabilitation ward'. This goes counter to the spirit of the recommendation and against the line of argument followed in Chapter 7. The professional training of Community Physicians, who have responsibility for planning, developing and coordinating services in Health Districts, and who would therefore play a key role in the Joint Mental Health Development Committees we have proposed, does not give appropriate priority to the psychiatric service sector.

General practitioners, more than most other professionals, can help to ensure continuity of care of patients as well as emergency help during 'unsocial hours'. They need to know which individuals in their practices are mentally ill or disabled and to be well acquainted with the care programmes planned for them.

General practitioners only become principals after a period of formal training, and the opportunity to teach the basic tenets of community care discussed in earlier chapters of this Report should be seized. The amount of time given to psychological and social problems has already increased and should be increased further.

Many principals will be eager to keep up with the latest ideas and it is important that the principles of community psychiatry should be included in the lectures and seminars for general practitioners given in the Medical Centres of District General Hospitals. General practitioners should be invited to take part in multidisciplinary training courses. Community psychiatric nurses can play a particularly important role, through their care of a practitioner's patients, in demonstrating the value of a broad community approach. There are now several group practices where a psychiatrist, psychologist, community psychiatric nurse, social worker, or counsellor are attached as regular visitors, both to see patients and for educational purposes. Such practices deserve special recognition.

Clinical psychologists are particularly skilled in assessment procedures, in designing programmes of rehabilitation and in supervising the application of techniques. Each day and residential unit should have access to the advice of a clinical psychologist on a sessional basis and all training courses will benefit from such specialist teaching. The education of clinical psychologists, in turn, should be based on a realistic appraisal of the value of these skills within an overall programme. It is rare that such procedures alone will effect a cure.

Occupational therapists and industrial supervisors carry out essential functions in a service for disabled people. The number of posts is inadequate and, in the case of industrial supervisors, the absence of training and a proper career structure is to be deplored. We suggest that specialist experience is just as important as for social workers and that some part of the training could well be taken in common with other mental health professionals.

Disablement Resettlement Officers and Hospital Resettlement Officers and the staff of Employment Rehabilitation Centres, Skillcentres and Remploy factories should be encouraged to visit community care units and discuss problems there, so that the close coordination of all the processes of care can be ensured.

Other professional groups include physiotherapists, speech therapists, lawyers, teachers, probation officers, the police and the clergy. All need to be aware of the special problems posed by the mentally ill or disturbed and of the way they can best contribute to an integrated process of community care. Even more important, those in charge of planning services need to understand how to use all professional groups to the advantage of disabled patients.

Voluntary agencies

The discussion in Chapter 6 indicates the value of taking over some of the attitudes of the staff of voluntary agencies into professional training. It also points to possible dangers that might come from *too* strict adherence to professional standards of education. One of the great advantages of voluntary bodies is that their staff do not (in general) count the hours, do not insist on protocol, do not create barriers between themselves and their clients; in a word, do not behave like professionals! Although this is not always true (there may be a point in the development of a voluntary service at which it becomes indistinguishable from a professional service), formal training courses can benefit greatly from the participation of teachers and students who do not subscribe enthusiastically to professional mores or rather, its negative aspects.

This is particularly true when members of self-help groups (patients and relatives) take part of their training in common with those taking more formal courses. The experience tends to break down stereotypes on both sides.

Summary

In this chapter we have suggested that the training of professional staff should be geared to the principles laid down in Chapter 7. Part, at least, of the training now provided, seems to have the aim of providing a rationale for the development of separate professions, even though much of the content of practice is not specific but common to all. On the other hand, particularly in social work, an insistence on 'generic' principles has led, not only to a claim for exclusive rights in non-specific procedures such as 'case-work', but to a rejection of the requirement, manifest to most other professions, to become expert in the knowledge and practice now available about mental illness.

We do not think it practicable to reverse this separation of the professions in the near future, but we suggest a number of ways in which disadvantages can be counteracted. The first is by better selection of recruits, on the basis of their likely ability to help patients or clients. The second is by requiring apprenticeship in multidisciplinary teams in an accredited district service. The third is by adequate specialisation, in the sense of specific training in the problems of the mentally disordered and disabled as well as in the wider academic lore of the particular profession concerned.

Social work and nursing are given detailed attention but the principles enunciated apply equally to medicine, clinical psychology or occupational therapy. The special contributions that voluntary workers can make are emphasised.

9 FINANCIAL IMPLICATIONS

Present spending patterns

We have now set out the arguments for a district service for the 'adult mentally ill', the local organisation of which would be planned and coordinated by a Joint Mental Health Development Committee containing senior representatives of local health and social services and representation from local voluntary organisations. The objective of this committee would be to bring the services at least up to the minimal quantitative standards (modified in conformity with local conditions) laid down in the 1975 White Paper (see Chapter 7, page 62), and to ensure that qualitative standards were established and maintained through the training and organisation of staff (see Chapter 8). Our proposals envisage that this Joint Committee should have a definable influence on the mental health budget.

Present spending patterns do not provide for, and are not moving towards, this concept of district responsibility for decent standards of community care. The provisional figures for 1980–81 show that £6755.4 millions were spent on Hospital and Community Health services (excluding primary health care). Of this sum, £692.4m. was allocated to mentally ill in-patients, £40.4m. for day-patients and £30.6m. for out-patients. The amount spent on all joint funding projects (not included in the total) was £37.6m.

The budget for Personal Social Services was £1677.5m. Residential care accounted for £673.1m. (£11.4m. for the mentally ill). Day care accounted for £184.2m. (£9.2m. for the mentally ill). Thus 2.4 per cent of the funds for residential and day care were spent on the mentally ill. Applying this proportion to the rest of the budget (for field social workers, home helps, meals on wheels, etc.) yields another £19.7m. for the mentally ill, making just over £40 million in all.

Thus only £111.3m., at most, was being spent on health and social services for the mentally ill, apart from in-patients; 1.3 per cent of the combined total budget. These figures do not include sickness benefits or welfare payments.

Some idea of the pitifully small provision made by local authorities is given in Table 9.1, which shows that only twelve mentally ill people per 100,000 population are being supported. If London is excluded, only one such individual receives help per ten thousand population.

Some indication of the speed of movement towards the minimal guidelines set out in the 1975 White Paper, and in The Way Forward,[7,8] can be obtained from the provisional figures for 1980-81 compared with expenditure during 1975-6, five years earlier. Data for day hospitals are not given. The figure for local authority residential accommodation was 0.11 per 1000 population compared with 0.10 per 1000 five years previously. At this rate of progress the lower guideline figure of 0.19 per 1000 would be reached in a further 40 years, ca. 2025 A.D. The figure for day care is given as 0.17 per 1000, compared with 0.10 five years earlier. The guideline of 0.60 would thus be reached, if this rate of increase were kept up, in 2011 A.D. In 1975, the then Secretary of State seemed to be pessimistic when suggesting that it would take a generation to reach even the minimum standards laid down. It seems, on the contrary, that she was being optimistic.

TABLE 9.1

Number of mentally ill residents supported by local authorities, by rate of 100,000 population aged 16–64, 31 March, 1981

Region	Total No.	Rate
Northern	176	9.1
Yorks/Humberside . .	301	9.9
North Western	468	11.7
West Midlands	298	9.2
East Midlands	169	7.1
London North	382	9.2
London	1356	31.5
Southern	287	7.2
South Western	73	3.7
England (Total)	3510	12.1

Source: DHSS. Personal Social Services. Local Authority Statistics. A/F81/11. Table E, p. 45 Amended.

We suggest, therefore, that a Development Fund should be set up, specifically in order to achieve a statutory requirement to establish proper qualitative and quantitative standards of community care. This would enable the JMHDCs to play a realistic role within their local districts. First, however, it would be necessary to identify the substantial sums already being spent by statutory authorities on specialist services for the mentally ill.

Identifying the present mental health budget

Every District Health Authority and every local authority Social Services Department should identify and publish its 'mental health' budget, covering both capital and revenue expenditure. We need not discuss the accounting procedures here but they would have to be specified in some detail so as to be comparable across districts. They should cover a period of perhaps ten years. Day and residential units and staff principally caring for the mentally ill would form the core resources in the calculation but a proportion of other expenses would need to be identified separately.

The Joint Mental Health Development Committee, other local bodies, the Regional authorities and the Department of Health and Social Security must be able to scrutinise the accounts item by item, compare them with those of other districts, compare the levels of service with those laid down, and elicit an explanation from any health or local authorities that are not meeting statutory requirements. The Joint Mental Health Development Committee, by reason of its senior membership, should be able to exercise an influence in the appropriate health and local authority committees. The Joint Mental Health Development Committee would produce an annual report on these matters, to be delivered to local District Health Authorities and Social Service Departments, Regional Health Authorities, the Department of Health and Social Security and the Inspectorate.

Publication of the details of baseline spending would also allow an assessment of whether any extra money received from the Development Fund was actually being spent on extra services, rather than on schemes that would otherwise have been covered by present funding arrangements. It would thus become possible for the Department of Health and Social Security planning committee, on the basis of local accounts, the Joint Mental Health Development Committee recommendations and applications, and reports from the Inspectorate, to allocate the Development Fund according to both need and merit. In this way, districts that provide a good service could be rewarded, so that centres of excellence would be built up as models for study and teaching, while districts that lag behind without good reason would find they were less able to attract extra funds.

The functions of the Joint Mental Health Development Committee would include the operation of the present joint funding arrangements whereby NHS money can be used to promote projects in the local authority and voluntary sectors.

It should also continue to be free to make separate applications for capital to the Housing Corporation, since many mentally ill people have a requirement for ordinary housing (including hostels, group homes, etc.) that is best met in this way.

A recent Department of Health and Social Security circular[10] has set out decisions on the suggestions made in the consultation document, Care in the Community. The circular still uses the term 'community' as a synonym for 'non-hospital'; a usage that we deplore because of the implication that people using hospital services are not in the community and cannot receive community care and that change to non-hospital services will *automatically* constitute an improvement.

Two useful decisions have been made. The first is to allow District Health Authorities to offer lump-sum payments or continuing grants to local authorities or voluntary organisations *for as long as necessary* in respect of identified in-patients transferred to alternative care. However, in many cases, particularly long-stay patients, the sum so transferred will not cover the higher costs of non-hospital care, and this may inhibit use of the arrangement. Moreover, we can foresee the possibility arising that local authorities will *only* be prepared to accept patients if the costs are transferred.

The second useful decision is that, in special circumstances, the arrangement whereby joint planning funds are tapered from three to seven years and then cut off, can be relaxed. Tapering can then begin at ten years and cut off at thirteen. District Health Authorities may, if they wish, continue to make payments even after thirteen years, but the money would have to come out of the ordinary budget. This decision only covers schemes 'aimed at enabling people to move out of hospital' and it remains to be seen how generously the term 'in special circumstances' will be interpreted. The problem that Social Service Departments will have to take an increasing responsibility for most new services from three years after joint funding begins, remains as before.

The joint finance allocations for 1983–4 have been somewhat in-increased and a small sum reserved for the support of pilot projects. Overall, the decisions announced in the circular should lead to a marginal improvement in services but they do not solve the large and urgent problems identified by the Enquiry. We think that much more substantial funds are necessary to cope with the present crisis in the mental health services.

A Development Fund for mental health services

The idea of a Development Fund is not new but previous efforts (including joint funding) to provide more money to extend the base for district mental health services have proved only partially successful and progress has been disappointingly slow. We suggest that this has been due to the lack of a grass roots organisation to assess local needs and to the difficulty local authorities have in taking over responsibility for the revenue costs for new services.

A Development Fund earmarked for the purpose of providing a solid basis of district services for the 'adult mentally ill' is the only way to overcome the present hiatus. Although similar in many ways to present joint financing (which should continue in parallel) it would not be restricted to schemes 'enabling people to move out of hospital' (since many of those in need are not in hospital) and funding would continue, if necessary, indefinitely.

Joint Mental Health Development Committees would make application for specified projects based on detailed knowledge of their districts, on the reports of the Inspectorate and on the advice of local monitoring bodies. Such funds would be used for both capital and revenue expenditure using the same mechanisms for disbursement as for the present joint funding but without the present tapering. Some districts would be allocated considerably more than the average; others considerably less.

Although we have used the term 'Development Fund' to designate this extra money, since it would indeed be used to build a foundation for real community care, we would not wish to say categorically that it would eventually be recouped from savings on the hospital service as the large old hospitals were run down and their remaining assets realised. The community service might well cost more to run than the old. If so, the Fund would eventually become routine expenditure. On the other hand, there clearly is a possibility that some of the money would eventually be recovered through real savings, as well as the sale of assets.

One further important advantage of our recommendation is that the needs of the 'single homeless' who are mentally ill or disabled could be met by making extra payments to those districts where the burden is greatest.

Allocating the Development Fund

It would be necessary for one of the Department of Health and Social Security ministers, assisted by a Departmental Planning Board, to be given special responsibility for the allocation of the Development Fund in order to improve and maintain the standards of community care for the mentally ill. Reports (including applications for funds) from Joint Mental Health Development Committees, the Inspectorate, District and Regional Health Authorities, and County and Borough Councils would provide information on which decisions would be based.

Public awareness

One of the major consequences and advantages of our proposal is that not only would those who provide the local community services and those who use them be given the opportunity to influence the way the services develop, but the publication of accounts would generate much public interest, both national and local. The interest would have a realistic basis because services would be matched against expenditure, but the aims and achievements of the local services could also be assessed.

Other mental health problems

We are concerned, in this Report, with the problems of the 'adult mentally ill'. The recommendations made could, however, be applied, with suitable modification, to the problems of the mentally retarded and elderly mentally infirm as well.

Summary

There is an overwhelming case for more provision to be made for the care and welfare of the mentally ill outside hospital. Present resources are inadequate even for minimum quantitative standards to be reached, let alone the improvement in quality of care (and, therefore, quality of life) that is universally agreed to be necessary.

We suggest that a Development Fund should be set up, to be disbursed under a named Department of Health and Social Security minister and Planning Board, through Regional Health authorities and the Joint Mental Health Development Committees described in Chapter 7 to District Health Authorities, Social Service Departments and voluntary bodies. This administrative structure, together with an Inspectorate, should have responsibility for seeing that minimum standards, both of quantity and of quality, are achieved.

The Joint Mental Health Development Committees would also scrutinise the capital and revenue expenditure of DHAs and SSDs over a ten year period in order to identify the amounts spent on the care and welfare of the mentally ill. These accounts would provide a basis for assessing future performance, since it would not be expected that, overall, the identified mental health budget should decrease, either absolutely or relatively. The accounts would also be available for public scrutiny and would allow the Department of Health and Social Security and Joint Mental Health Development Committees to judge the need (and likely effect) of allocating extra money from the Development Fund.

The present joint funding arrangements and the procedure whereby applications can be made to the Housing Corporation, should be transferred to the Joint Mental Health Development Committees.

DIAGRAM OF THE PROPOSED ORGANISATION OF
MENTAL HEALTH SERVICES

Department of Health
and Social Security
(Named Minister)

Regional
Health
Authorities

Social Service
Departments
(Counties and
Boroughs)

District   Voluntary   Social Service
Health   Organisations   Departments
Authorities   (District level)   (District level)

Joint Mental Health
Development Committees
(Districts)

Services in each District:
Residential and Day Units
Multidisciplinary Teams
Personal Care Coordinators

N.B.   (1) The Inspectorate would be concerned directly with the ser-
           vices in each District and reports would be sent to JMHDCs,
           DHAs, RHAs, SSDs and DHSS as well as to the service units.

       (2) There should be a mechanism through which voluntary
           bodies with a national organisation should be able to formu-
           late ideas and to exercise a coordinated influence on govern-
           ment policy.

10 CONCLUSIONS AND RECOMMENDATIONS

Summary of the problem facing the mental health service

Throughout this Enquiry we have encountered evidence that the age-long neglect of the mentally ill, although ameliorated by the infra-structure of the welfare state, by the statutory provisions of the National Health Service and Social Service Departments of the local authorities, and by the efforts of pioneering voluntary organisations, is still a marked feature of present-day society in Britain. In a recent survey of public attitudes it was discovered that people placed health at the top of a list of 20 personal priorities. Since mental health and physical health are so intricately linked that it is impossible to separate them, there is a clear contrast between public and private priorities.

The problem is compounded by 'swings of the pendulum': during the early Victorian period there was a swing away from the awful conditions of community care then prevailing, followed, after the pendulum had swung too far towards institutional care, and under the influence of the welfare reforms instituted after the second world war, by a swing back towards community care. In the view of members of the Enquiry, it is now in danger of swinging too far without the necessary input of resources. The large institutions, with their custodial history, their intimidating buildings, their overcrowded wards, and their atmosphere of isolation, in spite of everything that dedicated staff can do to improve the image, are 'running down'. The process has gone too far to consider refurbishing many of them. The serious problem for the mentally ill is that community care facilities have not been developed sufficiently to replace the functions that can no longer be undertaken by the large mental hospitals.

The 'mental health' services are therefore in a situation of crisis. Not only are they low on the list of public priorities but the efforts that have so far been made to improve the service have resulted in an erosion of their previous base without completing the construction of a new one.

Members of the Enquiry regard this position as intolerable and, in view of the international reputation Britain achieved for its pioneering developments during the 1950s, as reprehensible. Even in the present state of the economy, the case for measurably increasing the priority accorded to the mental health services is overwhelming.

91

Aims of mental health services

Services have two kinds of aims. They are intended to help all disabled people attain their fullest potential and to enhance their sense of personal worth, dignity and independence, and they try to provide forms of treatment and care that will prevent or ameliorate distress and disability. The term 'community care' is taken, in this Report, to mean that it is the responsibility of district services to see that these aims are achieved in so far as it is possible to do so. This responsibility includes the education and mobilisation of 'the community at large' to understand the plight of those who have broken down, are ill, or distressed and at risk, and to accept their solidarity with them; this means to give thought, time and energies and, where possible, hospitality, and to engage in friendship regardless of the content in which those in need of care may live their lives. We deplore the use of the term 'community care' as a slogan that diverts attention from the real issues of quality of life for mentally disordered, distressed or disabled people, whether or not they are living in 'institutions'.

Recommendations

The following recommendations stem directly from the argument in previous chapters. A reference is given for each so that the earlier discussion can be consulted for convenience. The order of the recommendations is approximately the reverse of their order in the text of the Report. It should be remembered that we are not here concerned with the severely mentally retarded or elderly mentally infirm, although many of the principles will apply also to them. The accompanying diagram gives a schematic idea of the organisation of services we propose.

1. STATUTORY OBLIGATIONS

The obligation placed on local health and social services under the Mental Health Act (1959) and the Health and Public Services Act (1968) should be reaffirmed by statute and the duty to see that it is implemented vested in a named Minister. Government policy, as frequently stated, is to provide a good quality of service within each geographical district so that large and remote mental hospitals can be closed. Unless this policy is reaffirmed and made mandatory it is unlikely to be achieved. This means that extra finance must be made available and appropriate local machinery set up to ensure minimum standards of care.

2. FINANCIAL

2.1 *The Development fund and its administration* (pp. 85—90)

A Development Fund should be set up under the control of a

designated minister working with a Departmental Planning Board. It would cover both capital and revenue expenses and would be earmarked specifically for the development of a wide spectrum of community services for the mentally ill. It would be administered in the same way as the current joint funding arrangements (which would continue in parallel), except that local authorities would not be expected to take over responsibility for funding from their own resources.

2.2 *Identifying the present mental health budget* (pp. 86—87)
The two major statutory authorities should be required to identify in detail what has been spent (both capital and revenue) on specialist services for the mentally ill for each district during the past ten years. This should be assessed against the levels of care actually provided and the particular problems of the district concerned. It would not be expected that overall expenditure (excluding contributions from the Development Fund) would drop, in real terms, during the next ten years, though this would vary according to the progress that had already been made.

3.   MAINTAINING STANDARDS
The quantitative standards laid down in the Government White Paper of 1975 are minimal but every district should aim at achieving at least these levels. Progress should be monitored through the proposed Joint Mental Health Development Committees and Inspectorate (paras. 4.2 and 4.5). Proper education of staff and volunteers is also essential (para. 6).

4.   ORGANISATION
4.1 *Principles* (pp. 57—58)
In order to achieve the aims of community care it is necessary for an organisation to be set up that will be responsible for identifying those in need in each district and meeting this need by planning comprehensive services (para. 4.2) and continuity of care. Geographical responsibility should be based on health districts, even when local authority boundaries are not contiguous. Provision should be made for alternative choices, for specialities requiring a larger population base, and for the needs of people without a 'parish of origin'.

4.2 *Joint Mental Health Development Committees* (pp. 68—69)
Every district should have a Joint Mental Health Development Committee, composed of senior representatives of local health, social and voluntary services, and led by a District Coordinator. Its duties should be as follows:

(i)   Achieving at least the statutory quantitative standards for the district community services, and improving their quality, irrespective of which administrative authority is responsible.

(ii) Scrutinising the mental health budget of the local health and social service authorities and comparing them with the service provided locally and with the budgets and services of other districts.

(iii) Operating the present joint funding arrangements through parent committees in the two statutory authorities.

(iv) Making applications for and disbursing, through the present authorities, money from the Development Fund.

(v)   Receiving and acting upon reports from the Inspectorate (para. 4.5).

(vi) Keeping in touch with staff teams so that information about the way most local needs are or are not being met is regularly updated.

4.3 *The administration of service units* (pp. 66—67)

Most service units should adopt operating policies that would make possible a comparison between aims and achievement. It is not appropriate for each unit to develop its own selection and treatment procedures irrespective of the overall pattern of services. On the other hand, most health and social services units should have greater autonomy in spending their budgets and in running their affairs in such a way as to achieve most effectively the agreed objectives. This would require considerable modification in the present hierarchical structure of professional nursing and social work, as well as in the way that units' budgets are now administered.

4.4 *Grass roots services* (p. 66)

Each individual in need should have access to a personal care co-ordinator familiar with the relevant circumstances of the case. This is only possible if all relevant staff, including those from voluntary organisations, are members of multidisciplinary teams. Experience in such teams should be regarded as an essential part of apprenticeship and training (para. 5). Personal care coordinators and teams should report, through whatever structure is appropriate in particular districts, to the JMHDCs, so that up-to-date information is always available concerning the match between need and services.

4.5 *Monitoring the mental health service* (pp. 69—70)

An Inspectorate should be set up to assess the achievements of service units compared with their aims. HM Inspectors of schools provide a model. Full use should also be made of Community Health Councils, Relative/Client/Staff Associations, Management Committees, and independent evaluative research. JMHDCs should be open to suggestions from all these sources.

5. COMPREHENSIVE COVERAGE (pp. 60—62)

The basic elements required in a comprehensive community service should be made mandatory. Apart from the units covered by this minimal requirement, innovations are needed to provide sheltered communities appropriate to modern conditions, day centres intermediate between 'occupational therapy' and 'sheltered workshops', high-level sheltered factories for the mentally ill, preparatory units where skills in every day living are taught, hostels that are available for refuge or rehabilitation as well as for treatment and, in general, provision for self-help and self-care in all units in order to foster independence. Some means must be found to get the agreement of unions who might otherwise feel that allowing disabled people to care and cook for themselves will deprive staff of a job.

6. EDUCATION

The problems faced by mentally ill people, and also posed by them, do not fit neatly into the curriculum of any one profession. The education of helping professionals is at the same time too general and too specific. It is too general because a professional training (for example social work) contains only a small content relevant to mental illness. It is too specific because a nurse does not learn enough about social work, or a psychologist about nursing, to understand how to collaborate in a multidisciplinary team or to act as a care coordinator. Selection and training of staff, and apprenticeship in a good community service, are the keys to improving the quality (as opposed to the quantity) of care. Part of the training should be taken in common. Detailed suggestions are made as to how the training of social workers and psychiatric nurses could be improved; the same principles apply to other professions.

7. ROLE OF VOLUNTARY ORGANISATIONS

Voluntary organisations may be active at both district and national level. In districts, their personnel should be able to take part as care coordinators and as members of multidisciplinary teams, and have the opportunity to be represented on Joint Mental Health Development Committees. At the national level, voluntary organisations with specialist skills to provide services for the mentally ill should be utilised by the Government to formulate policy. Amongst many other issues, anomalies such as, for example, Value Added Tax, which is not charged to local authorities but which voluntary organisations providing similar services have to pay, should be addressed.

ENVOI

by LORD LONGFORD

This has truly been a team effort. I was very fortunate in securing the participation of a Committee each of them fully qualified in their own right. The whole enterprise would have been impossible without the support of the Richmond Fellowship, who provided the essential facilities. I had long admired their unique work for the mentally afflicted under the inspiring leadership of Elly Jansen who, as Vice-Chairman, has made a special contribution to this Report. Our Committee are indebted to the Drafting Sub-Committee on whom fell much of the burden of the work in the later stages. The members were Lord Beswick, my colleague off and on for thirty years, Elly Jansen herself, Ken Coleman, the late Lord Redcliffe Maude and Professor Wing. The last-named played a pre-eminent part in the production of the Report. Willem van der Eyken, Development Officer of the Fellowship, was invaluable as Secretary.

Lord Redcliffe Maude left an ineffaceable impression on all who served with him, in this as in so many other spheres. He was already suffering from severe diabetes when he volunteered to serve on the Drafting Committee. He continued with us even after he was stricken with a fatal disease.

We all share a profound conviction that this sphere of social need has been hitherto scandalously neglected. There has been a disposition, perhaps understandable, to sweep the whole subject of mental illness under the carpet. Society has not only the duty to care for its vulnerable members but also to prevent mental illness, through recognition of the factors leading to breakdown, and acting on this understanding. We offer this Report as a contribution to a totally new approach and to a recognition that those labelled mentally ill cannot be separated off from the rest of us. We are all an indissoluble part of the human race.

REFERENCES

1. BARCLAY, P. M. (Chairman) (1982): *Social Workers: Their Role and Tasks*. London: Bedford Square Press.

2. BRANDON, D., PYKE-LEES, P., and WILDER, J. (1981): Voluntary organisations and rehabilitation. In: *Handbook of Psychiatric Rehabilitation Practice*. Eds: Wing, J. K., and Morris, B. Oxford: University Press.

3. BROWN, G. W., BONE, M., DALISON, B., and WING, J. K. (1966): *Schizophrenia and Social Care*. Oxford: University Press.

4. CENTRAL COUNCIL FOR EDUCATION AND TRAINING IN SOCIAL WORK (1974): *People with Handicaps need Better Trained Workers*. CCETSW Paper No. 5. Clifton House, Euston Road, London.

5. CHARITIES AID FOUNDATION (1982): Charity Statistics 1981/82.

6. CONWAY-NICHOLL, K., and ELLIOTT, A. (1982): North Camden community psychiatric nursing service. *British Medical Journal, 285,* 859–60.

7. DEPARTMENT OF HEALTH AND SOCIAL SECURITY (1975): *Better Services for the Mentally Ill*. Cmnd. 6233. London: HMSO.

8. DEPARTMENT OF HEALTH AND SOCIAL SECURITY (1977): *The Way Forward*. London: HMSO.

9. DEPARTMENT OF HEALTH AND SOCIAL SECURITY (1978): *The Government and the Voluntary Sector: A* Consultative Document. London: HMSO.

10. DEPARTMENT OF HEALTH AND SOCIAL SECURITY (1981): *Care in the Community: a Consultative Document on Moving Resources for Care in England*. See also DHSS Circular HC(83)6, LAC(83)5. London: HMSO.

11. EDWARDS, C., and CARTER, J. (1979): *Day services and the mentally ill*. In: *Community Care for the Mentally Disordered*. Eds: Wing, J. K., and Olsen, R. Oxford: University Press.

12. HOUSE OF LORDS (1981): Mental after-care. *Hansard 419,* 153–190.

13. HARTSHORN, A. E. (1982): *Milestones in Education for Social Work: The Carnegie Experiment, 1954–1958*. Dunfermline: Carnegie.

14. HOLLAND, S. (1979): The development of an action and counselling service in a deprived urban area. In: *New Methods of Mental Health Care*. (Ed.) Meacher, M. Oxford: Pergamon.

15. JANSEN, E. (Ed.) (1980): *The Therapeutic Community*. London: Croom Helm.

16. JONES, K. (1972): *A History of the Mental Health Services.* London: Routledge & Kegan Paul.

17. LEACH, J., and WING, J. K. (1980): *Helping Destitute Men.* London: Tavistock.

18. ROLLIN, H. (Ed.) (1980): *Coping with Schizophrenia: The National Schizophrenia Fellowship.* London: Burnet Books.

19. ROYAL COLLEGE OF GENERAL PRACTITIONERS (1981): *Prevention of Psychiatric Disorders in General Practice.* London: RCGP.

20. ROYAL COLLEGE OF PSYCHIATRISTS (1979): *Alcohol and Alcoholism. Report of a Special Committee.* London: Tavistock.

21. ROYAL COLLEGE OF PSYCHIATRISTS (1980): *Psychiatric Rehabilitation in the 1980s.* London: Royal College of Psychiatrists.

22. RYAN, P., and WING, J. K. (1979): Patterns of residential care: A study of hostels and group homes used by four local authorities to support mentally ill people in the community. In: *The Care of the Mentally Disordered: An Examination of some Alternatives to Hospital Care.* (Ed.) Olsen, R. Birmingham: BASW.

23. SHEPHERD, M., COOPER, B., BROWN, A. C., and KALTON, G. (1981): *Psychiatric illness in General Practice.* Second Edition. Oxford: University Press.

24. SIMS, A. (1981): The staff and their training. In: *Handbook of Psychiatric Rehabilitation Practice.* Eds: Wing, J. K., and Morris, B. Oxford: University Press.

25. UNELL, JUDITH (1979): *Voluntary Social Services: Financial Resources.* London: NCSS/PSSC.

26. WING, J. K. (1978): *Reasoning about Madness.* Oxford: University Press.

27. WING, J. K. (Ed.) (1982): *Long-term Community Care: Experience in a London Borough. Psychological Medicine.* Monog. Suppl. No. 2. Cambridge: University Press.

28. WING, J. K., and BROWN, G. W. (1970): *Institutionalism and Schizophrenia.* Cambridge: University Press.

29. WING, J. K., and MORRIS, B. (Eds) (1981): *Handbook of Psychiatric Rehabilitation Practice.* London: Oxford University Press.

30. WOLFENDEN (1978): *The Future of Voluntary Organisations. Report of the Wolfenden Committee.* London: Croom Helm.

INDEX